Culture, Language, and Curricular Choices

Culture, Language, and Curricular Choices

What Teachers Want to Know about Planning Instruction for English Learners

Edited by Mayra C. Daniel

ROWMAN & LITTLEFIELD
Lanham • Boulder • New York • London

Published by Rowman & Littlefield
A wholly owned subsidiary of The Rowman & Littlefield Publishing Group, Inc.
4501 Forbes Boulevard, Suite 200, Lanham, Maryland 20706
www.rowman.com

Unit A, Whitacre Mews, 26-34 Stannary Street, London SE11 4AB

Copyright © 2017 by Mayra C. Daniel

All rights reserved. No part of this book may be reproduced in any form or by any electronic or mechanical means, including information storage and retrieval systems, without written permission from the publisher, except by a reviewer who may quote passages in a review.

British Library Cataloguing in Publication Information Available

Library of Congress Cataloging-in-Publication Data Available

ISBN: 978-1-4758-2724-8 (cloth : alk. paper)
ISBN: 978-1-4758-2725-5 (pbk : alk. paper)
ISBN: 978-1-4758-2726-2 (electronic)

∞ ™ The paper used in this publication meets the minimum requirements of American National Standard for Information Sciences Permanence of Paper for Printed Library Materials, ANSI/NISO Z39.48-1992.

Printed in the United States of America

I dedicate this book to my colleague and friend Chris Liska Carger. Her zeal to help teachers explore students' funds of knowledge knew no bounds.

Contents

Foreword   ix
   Joan Wink

Preface   xiii

Acknowledgments   xvii

Introduction   xix

Part One: The Future of the Schoolhouse

1. Examining Components of School Districts with High Expectations for ELs' Academic Success   3
Ester de Jong and Tuba Yilmaz

2. Planning Instruction for ELs: Culture, Language, and the Curriculum   21
Mayra C. Daniel

3. Developing Bilingualism and Biliteracy in Content Instruction Using a Linguistic Integrative Perspective   37
Aida A. Nevárez-La Torre

Part Two: Considerations for Examining and Supporting Language Development

4 Language Is a Resource: Revaluing Readers' Transliteracies through Miscue Analysis and Retrospective Miscue Analysis (RMA)   59
Yetta Goodman and Kelly Allen

5 Language Development in Early Readers and Writers   87
Carol Owles

6 Exploring English Learners' Languages and Cultures through Visual Literacy   101
Mayra C. Daniel

Part Three: Authentic Data-Driven Evaluation

7 Considerations for Instruction and Assessment of ELS with Special Educational Needs   121
Barbara E. Marler

References   135

About the Editor   149

Contributors   151

Foreword

Joan Wink

Dear readers, how clever of you to have grabbed this book at this moment in time. You will not regret it, I promise. It is an honor to introduce you to Mayra Daniel, her perceptive coauthors, and their wise and critical content in each of these chapters.

Language teachers, this one is for you, and we are all language teachers, even if we think we are math, or secondary, or history, or science teachers. Language is what we all have in common, even when we teach specific content or age groups. The world has changed, and today we have students who bring many languages into our classes. None of us can do this alone—it takes us all.

Before I let you know about all of the treasures you are going to find within these pages, I have a story.

I will never forget the first time I met Mayra Daniel. It was late afternoon on the East Coast in early March, and it was dark, dreary, and damp. I had been running from session to session all day at an international convention, and I was exhausted but not yet finished with the long day.

A warm cup of soup was on my mind as I trudged off to one final session. It is true that I was also thinking of a glass of wine. However, I had a bilingual interest section meeting, which I just could not miss. I had been a part of this group for many years, and I know that every voice counts. In the last few years our small interest section had been struggling, so I felt even more determined not to skip out on this annual meeting. Frankly, however, I was not too optimistic.

I entered the room, and there were only a few weary, committed souls there. Hugs of camaraderie filled the room. Suddenly, a lively young woman entered, and the entire atmosphere changed. I thought: Who is this person who brings such energy and interest? It was Mayra, and she also brought friends, colleagues, and newcomers with her. I knew immediately that the sun had come out for our previously struggling group.

New blood. Energy. Action. Yes, this is what I had been waiting for with this group for several years. Mayra brought not only energy but also expertise. Since that time, I have had the pleasure of working with Mayra on various writing projects, and I have learned that she, indeed, is one of those colleagues who shows up early and doesn't leave until all the chairs are returned, the empty coffee cups tossed, the chart paper taken down from the wall, and the ideas captured in notebooks or computers. She stays until the Is are dotted and the Ts are crossed.

This book is written *by* reflective and theoretically grounded practitioners who bring complex understandings of bilingualism, multilingualism, and translingualism. These authors have lived their lives in the context of lots of different languages. The book is *for* teachers, beginners and experienced, who want to know how to plan and why those plans are effective, when classrooms have speakers of other languages.

First, Mayra and her colleagues take us into the schoolhouse (part 1) of today and tomorrow where the efficacy of learning environments and high expectations (chapter 1, de Jong and Yilmaz) for *all* students, particularly those who enrich the classroom with languages in addition to English, has the highest priority. In chapter 2, Mayra lays a solid foundation with her deep knowledge of the many connections between language and culture. Nevárez-La Torre (chapter 3) helps readers understand how to focus on specific content instruction with kids who speak and understand other languages.

In the second part of the book, Yetta Goodman and Kelly Allen (chapter 4) make visible the notion of language orientations and language as a resource through miscue and retrospective miscue analysis. From here, Owles (chapter 5) expands on the importance of respecting and nurturing each student's unique path to learning with specific instructional approaches, which are grounded in culturally responsive instruction. Part 2 ends with Mayra (chapter 6) sharing her understandings of visual literacy and scaffolding in an additive approach to theory and practice of multilingualism.

The book concludes with a research-based approach (part 3, chapter 7 by Marler) to the instruction and assessment of students who find themselves in the intersection of bilingualism and/or special education.

Mayra and her colleague are teachers, scholars, and researchers; in addition, they are leaders in the area of making meaning of language and content as the world changes rapidly. As you walk into your schoolhouse of today and tomorrow, this knowledge of language acquisition will strengthen and enrich the school community, the local community, and our shared national community.

Are you wondering what became of Mayra since I met her years ago at the interest section meeting? Since that time, her knowledge and leadership has guided that interest section, and she has risen through the ranks of leadership in the international organization. See, I told you—*language teachers lead*. It has been said that followers choose leaders, and I am happy to say that I am now one of Mayra Daniel's followers.

Preface

A career as a teacher requires a commitment to the future of our world. It is a choice made by the individual who believes that learning how to do anything well demands careful attention to the implicit factors of the object of study. The authors whose chapters you will read write for the caring educator, for the new and the more experienced practicing teacher, and for the teacher candidate who wants to explore new ways of designing and delivering instruction.

Good teachers care about their work and want to gain in pedagogical expertise throughout their careers. They are the people who attend a party and think about ways to use the hats and whistles left behind by the guests as props to engage their students in future lessons. The thoughts shared by the contributors to this book are for educators who want to know (1) how to plan instruction for their English learners (ELs) and (2) the reasons the instructional strategies they have been encouraged to implement are effective.

We know that teachers advocate for all learners when they investigate ELs' funds of knowledge (Owles, ch. 5) and plan culturally responsive instruction (Daniel, ch. 2). Educators know that no one teacher can have mastery of all the languages spoken by their students' families and communities, yet they want to plan lessons that serve to showcase the learners' knowledge. They are intrigued when they observe what multilingual students do to make meaning in their classrooms.

All chapter authors present a unified perspective: first, that it is essential to recognize that ELs hold knowledge before they come to school and, secondly, that ELs' cultures and languages will enrich and strengthen this nation's citizenry. Their overarching goal is to address topics that will support teachers in their continued exploration of the impact of language development on learning.

There is an unspoken message across the chapters in this book that educators at all levels have unanswered questions about transliteracy development. These questions merit exploration. We propose that current philosophies of literacy do not provide absolute and complete understandings of the plurilingual language acquisition process. We believe that all educators who work with ELs must continue to examine the translingual nature of multiliteracy development.

Our conversations with you center on instructional practices that will energize you to open doors to link the school curriculum to the learners' homes (deJong & Yilmaz, ch. 1). We encourage you to develop an awareness that translingual literacy methodology is in its infancy, and that an interest in exploring literacy processes will lead you and your colleagues to ask and find answers to important questions.

Chapter authors are lifelong learners committed to innovation in the classroom. They are educators whose work with ELs led them to question educational paradigms and theories of language acquisition. Their observations of what students do to understand content taught in a language they are working to learn lead them to identify and recommend effective pathways for instruction.

The authors' work takes them outside the university environment to K–12 classrooms that represent the current demographic of students enrolled in U.S. schools. In their chapters, they provide a theoretical and research-based rationale that is based on the *language as a resource* philosophy. Students' home languages are identified as a scaffold to teach discipline specific concepts and language. Educating ELs begins with respecting their pluriliteracies and examining students' literacy processes for how these showcase their learning (Goodman & Allen, ch. 4).

Teachers strive to engage in inquiries that help them and their colleagues grow professionally in situated practice (Nevárez-La Torre, ch. 3). They hope to decrease sociocultural mismatches between educational institutions and the ELs' communities. They want parents to know that many educators are making efforts to learn about ELs' plurilingual and pluricultural backgrounds.

No educator expects that top-down mandates from the U.S. Office of Education will cease anytime soon. Regardless of which political party has the greater number of members in the U.S. Congress, ELs will continue to need culturally and linguistically responsive instruction. This educational need mandates that teachers' instructional planning considers who the learners are and what knowledge base they bring to school.

The strategic teaching methods in this book are relevant to teaching ELs across time (Daniel, ch. 6). As you examine ideas presented, you will create interpretations that inform instructional planning and only allow room to conduct fair evaluation of ELs (Marler, ch. 7). We propose to empower teachers to influence district- and school-level policies as they guide ELs to academic achievement.

Contributing authors are teacher trainers who have crossed personal and professional borders during their lives. They have all worked with teachers in the United States and other countries. Their stories reflect experiential and academic knowledge. Their histories permeate their teaching philosophies and empower them to advocate for social justice in the schoolhouse. Their beliefs evidence lives of cultural conflict, personal and familial survival, and ultimate triumph. Their words evidence that it is possible for the schoolhouse to nurture all learners to become the future leaders of our nation.

This book is the first in a series of two written for teachers who want to learn all they can about working with ELs. The conversation begun in *Culture, Language, and Curricular Choices: What Teachers Need to Know about Planning Instruction for English Learners* will continue in a book titled *Taking English Learners to the Head of the Class*.

Acknowledgments

I want to recognize all of you who worked with me on this project for your commitment to excellence.

I hear the empowering message that the contributing authors send to teachers. At this time in U.S. history, your words hit the bullseye. You encourage educators to think outside the box. You show us that we must applaud the cultural and linguistic diversity present in our schools and communities. Thank you for the reminder that this country's democratic system begins in kindergarten.

A big thank-you to Tom Koerner for suggesting that what I thought would be one book should become two and for his guidance preparing this manuscript. Thanks also to Carlie Wall and to Suzanne Canavan from Rowman & Littlefield. What a great team!

Introduction

As immigration to a country increases, the number of first-generation children rises proportionately. The U.S. educational system is working to address the educational needs of both new arrivals and children of immigrant parents born within this nation. Educating these learners is an ongoing challenge for the largely monolingual teacher workforce in this country, as it is not unusual for teachers to have several nationalities represented in their classroom.

Chapter authors believe that all students have the right to literacy instruction that honors their languages, validates their funds of knowledge, and acknowledges their cultural capital. Because literacy is both social and cultural, effective instructional models require that teachers accept language use that incorporates transliteracy and considers translanguaging natural parts of language acquisition.

Committed educators want to know more about how English learners (ELs) negotiate meaning. When they take time to explore the language(s) students use to communicate outside of school, they are prepared to advocate for students' experimentation with language rather than focus on the errors they might make.

While several culture groups may share a language, geographical differences influence the way languages evolve and the communication of its speakers. For example, English and Spanish can be quite different when spoken in the Americas or Europe. Depending on the continent and the person's communicative needs, individuals interact using colloquialisms, nouns, and expressions that reflect the particular country's history and economic climate.

In *Culture, Language, and Curricular Choices: What Teachers Need to Know about Planning Instruction for English Learners*, the authors address issues of language diversity and also go beyond these to emphasize the impact of culture on the learning environment. In addition to the many languages ELs bring to U.S. schools, students today evidence a plethora of schooling and home experiences.

Teachers need to identify and teach the background knowledge that is unique to the United States to ensure the ELs understand the context of instruction. The authors write for educators who want to investigate students' communities and better understand ELs' familial networks.

This book is written for teachers and school administrators who understand that the schoolhouse has to address a student demographic that is plurilingual and pluricultural. It is for school administrators who want to encourage EL expertise and teacher leadership in their districts.

ORGANIZATION OF THIS BOOK

The chapters in *Culture, Language, and Curricular Choices* are organized into three parts:

Part 1: The Future of the Schoolhouse. In this section the authors take the reader on a path to examine the *language as a resource philosophy* (Ruiz, 1984). They encourage teachers to consider the *complexity of transliteracy processes* and to widen the scope of their pedagogical practices. This section begins the teachers' journey to explore a *pedagogy of equity* that validates all learners' realities.

Part 2: Considerations for Examining and Supporting Language Development. Continuing the goals of part 1, the authors present a vision of an equitable schoolhouse where valuing plurilingual learners is the norm. Understanding how to aid ELs negotiate their pluricultural identities supports their social-emotional learning and language development. Examples of what teachers can do are replicable and will help teachers design similar tasks.

Part 3: Authentic Data-Driven Evaluation. Contrived and controlled interventions, focused on discreet areas of skill or concept attainment, are not authentic measures of students' knowledge. The objective of this section is to emphasize why effective collaboration is needed between teachers and members of response to intervention (RTI) evaluation teams.

CONTENT OF EACH CHAPTER

The message in this book is for the caring and reflective educator. The authors engage teachers in a conversation that seeks to foster their leadership potential. Their focus encourages teachers to examine the challenges and successes they experience in their work with today's highly diverse student demographic. The chapters in this book focus on improving instruction in schools and creating culturally responsive communities of learning. The components of each chapter are as follows:

1. The *initial presentation* of the topic to be discussed is found in a few sentences before each chapter's narrative begins. This offers the reader a quick glimpse of what the chapter author will cover.
2. The reader is then introduced to the *rationale or conceptual framework* that supports the recommendations for practice that will be shared in section 3. Chapter authors present their arguments for strategies that teachers might follow to plan instruction in classrooms with ELs. The objective of this section is to provide information that will support teachers' curricular innovations.
3. In *practical applications for the classroom*, writers focus on identifying and presenting examples of the lesson components that are needed to design culturally responsive instruction.
4. The *recommendations* section of each chapter presents additional options for planning classroom instruction that teachers may want to investigate.
5. The last section, *resources*, is developed by each author as best fits the topic of each chapter. Some writers shared resources for teachers, others technology resources, and yet others listed both suggestions for materials to use in lesson planning and examples of up-to-date current technologies.

Part One

The Future of the Schoolhouse

Chapter One

Examining Components of School Districts with High Expectations for ELs' Academic Success

Ester de Jong and Tuba Yilmaz

Actions at the district, school, and classroom level affect how schools create effective learning environments for culturally and linguistically diverse students. The authors identify key district policies, features of school leadership, and principles of effective classroom practices, including those that affirm ELs' identities, embrace a language-as-resource perspective, and engage ELs in a high-quality curriculum with high expectations.

Linguistic and cultural diversity is the norm in American schools. Almost one quarter of students in U.S. schools speak a language other than English at home; about 9 percent of all K–12 students nationwide are also English language learners (OELA, 2015). Effective educators view this diversity as a resource rather than a problem (Ruiz, 1984). When it comes to the schooling experiences of ELs, the language-as-resource orientation aims to reframe competence in a minority language from being perceived as deficits (or problems) to being viewed as individual and social assets. Effective systems engage in language-in-education (LIE) policy-making and practices that reflect this stance. We conceptualize language policy as a layered process where teacher, school, district, state, and national policies interact and intersect to collectively create learning environments for ELs (Ricento & Hornberger, 1996).

Formal, explicit state or national government policy documents often set the parameters and the tone for implementation at other policy levels, such as the district and the school level; however, further negotiation and interpretation emerge at the other levels. Although Ricento and Hornberger (1996) emphasize school rather than district policies, the latter also play an important role. Programs for ELs are often coordinated at the district level; districtwide policies are subsequently implemented and interpreted at the school level. Finally, teachers and their interpretation and enactment of language policies are at the core of language policy processes. After all, teachers affect "the ways educational reforms are enacted, mediated, and shaped in the classroom" (Stritikus, 2002, p. 17; Olsen & Kirtman, 2002).

For the purpose of this chapter we will focus on the institutional and interpersonal levels of decision-making for ELs. In particular, the chapter focuses on the following areas: (1) developing districtwide EL expertise; (2) school-based leadership; and (3) effective classroom practices. The reader is referred to the following resources that provide historical reviews and analyses of federal and state policies in the United States (Gándara & Hopkins, 2010; Ovando, 2003; Wiese & García, 1998).

DISTRICTWIDE DECISION-MAKING FOR ELS

Traditionally, little attention has been given to district-level policies and practices and how these shape the schooling experiences of ELs. Yet guidelines for program entry and exit of ELs, for curriculum adoption and materials, and for professional development are typically set at the district level (Ragan & Lesaux, 2006). Moreover, expertise and leadership matters greatly at this level as it connects to vision and funding (Elfers & Stritikus, 2013; Reyes & Garcia, 2014). A study by de Jong, Gort, and Cobb (2005), for example, illustrates how district leadership's vision of effective instruction shaped their interpretation of a restrictive language law (Massachusetts' Question 2). The districts had a long history of successful bilingual education programs and the program leaders found ways to construct implementation spaces (Hornberger, 2002) that supported a more bilingual stance. Coleman and Goldenberg (2010) stress the importance of coherent and consistent districtwide policies within a system of clearly defined goals and ways to document success.

Horwitz and colleagues (2009) studied the policies and practices of four different successful districts (Dallas, New York City, San Francisco, and St. Paul) and analyzed the historical, administrative, and programmatic structures of the schools in these districts to explain the growth in EL achievement. They found that these four districts employed several strategies to increase EL success, including extensive and continuous support for implementation, a culture of collaboration and shared accountability across decision-making levels, hybrid models of instructional management and local empowerment, strategic school staffing, and the strategic use of EL funds. The study also highlighted that effective districts integrate an EL focus throughout their professional development efforts.

This study underscores the importance of ensuring that expertise has a voice when decisions about curriculum, assessment, and professional development are being made at the district level. It also shows that EL-related expertise needs to be distributed at all decision-making levels, from the classroom to the superintendent's leadership council. District-level personnel also perform an important role as mentors and advocates for access to services across the school system (Torres-Guzmán & Goodwin, 1995).

SCHOOLWIDE PRACTICES

The institutional level also includes school-based decision-making. One basic decision is how to organize services for ELs: what does the program look like? Is there a bilingual education program that uses the students' native language and English; or an English as a second language (ESL) program? Regardless of the model that best fits the student population, resources, and program goals, however, effective programs for ELs are fully integrated in the school. Such schoolwide integration does not mean that all ELs are placed full-time in mainstream classrooms; it does imply that collaborative structures are in place and that decisions are made with ELs in mind rather than treating ELs as an afterthought. Abu El-Haj (2006) refers to this as "substantive inclusion" (p. 190), and this principle implies full participation and inclusion of all the components in a school (de Jong, 2011).

Other practices to provide equitable learning environments include professional development activities for all students, communications to parents, promotional materials, and fundraising endeavors (Scanlan & Palmer, 2009). A classic study by Carter and Chatfield (1986) on an effective elementary school, Lauderbach, explains this inclusive school culture: "Lauderbach is an effective school with an effective bilingual program. The bilingual program is not a separate part of the school but rather participates in, partakes of, and contributes to the positive student and educational climate outcomes" (p. 226).

Schoolwide practices begin with leadership that is deeply knowledgeable about effective schooling for linguistically and culturally diverse students (Brooks, Adams, & Morita-Mullaney, 2010; López & Iribarren, 2014; Mace-Matluck, 1990). Principals need to be able to advocate for appropriate services and equity in resources, work with the ELs' parents, and establish organizational structures that support program and staff integration. Reyes and Garcia (2014) investigated a culturally responsive principal's initial practices to transform a failing school with a high Latino/a population into an achieving school. The five main changes the principal made were: 1) prepare a welcoming, multilingual school atmosphere; 2) raise student achievement; 3) start a dual language bilingual program; 4) provide extracurricular opportunities to all students; and 5) increase parental involvement.

School-based management also encourages that school leaders make decisions about professional development; effective schools engage in effective professional development for all teachers that include the needs of ELs, not only the ESL or bilingual teacher. Carrejo, Cortez, and Reinhartz (2010), for example, describe how principals improve ELs' achievement in science through a community of practice approach to professional development.

Collaboration among teachers is another component of an integrated school. Teachers can modify the curriculum collaboratively to increase the effectiveness of the accommodations, and co-teach to share responsibility and to maximize teacher and student growth (Beninghof & Leensvaart, 2016). Multiple models for collaboration between paraprofessionals and mainstream teachers, between ESL and bilingual teachers and mainstream teachers have emerged to best meet the needs of ELs (Honigsfeld & Dove, 2010). When there is a separate program for ELs (such as a bilingual program or a self-contained ESL program), collaboration is also important to ensure sociocultural student integration and opportunities for cultural and linguistic exchange (de Jong, 2006; López & Iribarren, 2014).

CLASSROOM PRACTICES

As noted, teachers are at the core of practices. Effective teaching for linguistically and culturally diverse students requires specific approaches to pedagogy, curriculum, and assessment. While studies have highlighted a wide range of practices, effective approaches to teaching and learning for ELs can be characterized with a few core principles: (1) affirm ELs' identities; (2) embrace a language-as-resource perspective; and (3) engage ELs in a high-quality curriculum with high expectations (Brisk, 2008; de Jong, 2011). We will focus the remainder of this chapter on these principles and will highlight specific practices in the next section. Practices that align with these principles increase ELs' academic engagement and achievement.

Affirming Identities

Lucas and Villegas (2013) refer to the importance of linguistically and culturally responsive teaching practices to create safe, effective, and equitable learning environments for ELs and to give them a sense of belonging. Culturally responsive instruction encourages teachers to establish different and varied instructional classroom strategies to meet EL students' needs with a critical perspective (Kumashiro, 2004; Li, 2012; Nzai, Gomez, Reyna, & Jen, 2012). It is based on caring instruction, which requires respect and value to diversity (Noddings, 1984; Valenzuela, 1999), and fair teaching, which includes equitable access to resources and curriculum that reflect diverse students' living realities (Carrasquillo & Rodriguez, 1998; Gorski, 2013).

Getting to know your ELs as bi/multilingual learners plays a substantial role to provide effective instruction to ELs. Carrasquillo and Rodriguez (1998) observed students in two elementary schools and one high school in New York City. Their study revealed that a focus on the whole student valued and respected ELs' personal experiences and cultures and contributed to higher levels of student achievement. In their study with 110 Spanish-speaking middle schoolers, García and Chun (2016) explored the influence of the culturally responsive teaching practices and teacher expectations on academic achievement. The results indicated teachers' high expectations and diverse teaching practices had a positive effect on academic self-efficacy and academic performance.

Assessment also plays an important role in affirming students' academic and linguistic identities. Assessment in and across both languages and ongoing formative assessments are needed to identify ELs' strengths and academic and linguistic needs. This allows teachers to recognize ELs' successes overtly and frequently, to differentiate instruction, and to provide appropriate feedback. Targeted accommodations of assignments support student achievement (Kopriva, Emick, Hipolito-Delgado, & Cameron, 2007).

Gold (2006) analyzed six effective bilingual programs in California and found that the school staff cooperatively examined the progress of each EL through portfolios and rosters to address their needs and to provide them scaffolding in different ways. In addition, teachers continued to work on raising expectations for all students to master grade-level standards, and enhance ELs' cognitive processing. Student progress is monitored through ongoing, systematic student assessments, which involves not only standardized tests but also the formative assessments, writing samples, oral reading episodes, summaries of texts to demonstrate comprehension, and so forth (Coleman & Goldenberg, 2010). These tools provide teachers timely information about how students are progressing with respect to defined academic goals, and what kind of modifications should be done on instructional strategies.

Language as Resource Perspective

A consistent principle underlying effective schools for ELs is that their schooling is approached from a language-as-resource perspective (Ruiz, 1984). This perspective views the linguistic and cultural diversity that students bring to school as an asset rather than a problem or deficit. Practices that support the students' native language use and development are key for the success of ELs. These practices leverage the entirety of the cognitive, linguistic, and cultural resources that students bring to the learning task, not just those that can only be seen or expressed through the students' second language.

Rodríguez and colleagues (2012) found in their study with twenty-eight ELs that the students who received computer-based first-language support had significantly higher scores in the area of reading comprehension. Similarly, Lucero (2014) found in her study that teachers facilitated academic language development by providing oral linguistic scaffolding for emergent bilingual students at both the micro and macro levels. Palmer and colleagues (2006) revealed that when the teacher viewed the ELs' primary language as an asset and encouraged students to keep using Chinese while developing their English reading, writing, listening, and speaking skills, the level of biliteracy, biculturalism, and bilingualism among students was increased. While not every district or school can implement strong dual language education programs, every teacher can take an additive bilingual stance (de Jong & Freeman, 2010). That is, they view the students' home and community language as a resource to extend and build on, not as something that needs to be eradicated or replaced.

High-Quality, Equitable Learning Environments

Teachers can motivate, encourage, support, and expect high degrees of efforts and accomplishments from the ELs by providing a challenging and theme-based curriculum that promotes high standards and helps ELs develop academic concepts and higher thinking skills (Freeman, Freeman, & Mercuri, 2003; Li, 2012). In addition to being culturally relevant, a high quality curriculum encourages creativity and critical thinking for ELs at all levels of second language proficiency (Galguera & Hakuta, 1997; Thompson, 2004), and provides equitable learning environments on the contrary of the subtractive belief that ELs should not be challenged due to their limited English proficiency (Li, 2012).

High expectations need to be accompanied, however, by extensive scaffolding strategies that support ELs' learning (August & Shanahan, 2006; Coady, Hamann, Harrington, Pacheco, Pho, & Yedlin, 2008). Given the diversity of ELs in terms of their educational background and cultural experiences, as well as their immigrant experience, the skilled teacher of ELs differentiates instruction without lowering expectations.

PRACTICAL APPLICATIONS

In classrooms where ELs demonstrate a high level of academic achievement, teachers create a welcoming classroom atmosphere where ELs' cultures and background knowledge are valued and employ teaching strategies that differentiate instruction based on students' needs, that make content more comprehensible for ELs, and that modify the curriculum in ways that scaffold rather than lower expectations for ELs. In this section, we highlight examples of specific practices in support of the three principles above: affirming identities through identity texts and critical autobiographies; maintaining high expectations by scaffolding instruction; using and extending students' native language resources through bilingual books and dialogue journals; and building relationships among students from diverse backgrounds through cooperative learning.

Identity Texts and Critical Autobiographies

To engage bilingual learners in a wide range of literacy activities that draw on the linguistic and cultural resources learners bring to school, teachers can have students write dual language books or *identity texts* (Cummins et al.,

2005). An example of these texts is described in a multilingual literacies project implemented by monolingual English-speaking teachers working in linguistically and culturally diverse English-medium schools in Toronto (Bernhard et al., 2006; Cummins et al., 2005). Students were invited to write about topics that are aligned with the regular content-area instruction in English and their heritage language. Teachers organize students into same language groups (e.g., bilingual Urdu/English speakers in one group, bilingual Bengali/English speakers in another group), and students drew on each other's' language and literacy strengths in English and their heritage language to write their books in two languages. Publication on the Web facilitates students' development of computer literacies and allows the books to reach a wider audience.

Critical autobiographies are another example of culturally responsive practices that allow students to examine events in their lives that affect them as bilingual individuals (Brisk, Burgos, & Hamerla, 2004; Brisk & Harrington, 2000). In this project-based approach to teaching, students describe their lives as bilingual-bicultural learners and then connect their life stories to social, political, economic, cultural, and linguistic events. The project is student-centered and learning occurs through discussion and the reading of a wide range of fiction and nonfiction books. Critical autobiographies allow students to explore their own identities, and they provide an authentic context for language and literacy development.

Scaffolding Instruction

Effective teachers of ELs use a wide range of strategies to ensure access to the content, including making instruction comprehensible, questioning techniques, and maintaining explicit attention to academic language and literacy development (Calderon, Slavin, & Sanchez, 2011; Deussen et al., 2008; de Jong & Harper, 2005; Islam & Park, 2015). English-language learners need simultaneous access to content and language development. To make content more accessible, effective teachers use strategies to make their input (oral and written text) more comprehensible. To this end, teachers can use graphic organizers, charts, objects, manipulative materials, visuals, maps, and non-verbal cues, including gestures, facial expressions, and physical responses (Echevarria, Vogt, & Short, 2014). Effective teachers use questioning techniques that are sensitive to the ELs' stage of language production, yet also encourage critical thinking, even for ELs at the lower proficiency levels (de Jong & Derrick-Mescua, 2003; Hill & Flynn, 2008).

It is insufficient, however, to only shelter the content; ELs must also develop the social and academic language to function in their classrooms and the wider (school) community. To this end, teachers need to pay explicit attention to how they create opportunities for students to hear, see, and use academic language in meaningful contexts (Gersten et al., 2007; Zwiers, 2007). They also need to pay attention to how they provide feedback. Research in language immersion classrooms shows that there is a role for a focus on form to scaffold the mastery of specific linguistic features (Lyster, 2004).

Using the Native Language

Effective teachers strategically use students' native language resources for multiple purposes, such as clarifying and assessing content learning, building social relationships, teaching key concepts, and making cross linguistic connections (Gersten & Baker, 2000; Tikunoff & Vazquez-Faria, 1982). Many refer to the practice of strategically using multilingual resources as a pedagogical tool as "translanguaging" (Celic & Seltzer, 2011; García & Yip, 2015; Li, 2012). Translanguaging as a teaching pedagogy views language learners as members of the classroom community and values their bilingual/bicultural identities. Importantly, even monolingual teachers can engage in bilingual practices—this is not the exclusive domain of bilingual teachers (de Jong, 2013).

Bilingual and monolingual mainstream and ESL/bilingual teachers can use a range of strategies to build on students' native languages. Among others, they can acquire and use bilingual books (Ernst-Slavit & Mulhern, 2003), create multilingual signs, encourage students to use their native language when discussing content in writing (Haneda & Wells, 2012; Reed & Railsback, 2003), and share in the process of learning another language themselves. Hesson, Seltzer, and Woodley (2014) add the use of bilingual dictionaries and cognate charts as additional strategies.

Cooperative Learning

Cooperative learning has proven to be a key strategy in diverse classrooms. It provides various opportunities and scaffolding to practice the language, increase student-student interaction, and build rapport among students who work for a common goal (Berg, Petrón, & Greybeck, 2012; Deussen et al., 2008; Nzai et al., 2012; Pease-Alvarez, García, & Espinosa, 1991; Reed &

Railsback, 2003). Mohan (1990) revealed that the amount of speaking time and the quality of the ELs' talk in L2 increase in cooperative learning environments where ELs and mainstream students negotiate meaning, discuss the material, exchange information on academic content, and collaborate on the assigned projects. Curtin (2005) identified some of the challenges that ESL students experienced as they mainstreamed into regular classrooms after spending one or two years in a sheltered ESL classroom. The results indicated that ELs were more comfortable and more confident with teaching styles that were more interactive and that required cooperation among ELs and mainstream students.

Cooperative learning structures for academic or social language development require more than mere opportunities to interact in the target language. While exposure to the target language in cooperative work is valuable, it should be supported with explicit academic instruction and preparation techniques in order to also support language development (de Jong & Harper, 2005). De Jong & Lopez Estrada (2011), for example, found that even a simple structure such as think-pair-share (in which the teacher asks a question, students think and turn to a partner to share their answer, and then share out) requires that teachers consider pre-teaching key vocabulary, provide sentence frames for students at beginning proficiency levels so they can participate, and purposefully work to extend student language output.

CONCLUSIONS AND RECOMMENDATIONS FOR ACTION

Educators are language decision-makers. Whether at the national, state, district, school, or classroom level, educational and language policies shape our daily language practices. To bring this awareness to the task of schooling ELs is an important first step. Another next step is to bring agency to this task and actively create implementation spaces that support ELs in meeting academic, language and literacy, and sociocultural goals. In this chapter, we have focused on three levels where decision-makers can have a direct and positive impact on ELs: the district, the school, and the classroom level. Based on this framework, we recommend the following actions:

Districts

1. Develop and access EL expertise at all levels throughout the district, including input into curriculum development and professional development
2. Develop coherent and systemic approaches to the schooling of ELs that are sensitive to differences in needs and resources while striving for common high-level outcomes

Schools

- Build and support strong leaders who are knowledgeable about effective schooling for ELs
- Prepare all teachers to work with English learners
- Integrate students, staff, and programs within the school structure
- Build collaborative structures that support on-going professional development as well as classroom practices

Teachers

- Be prepared to engage in practices that affirm students' identities, build on and extend students' linguistic resources, and maintain high expectations

Online Resources for Practical Ideas

Identity texts: Go to http://thornwood.peelschools.org/Dual/ for detailed description of this process and examples of student-made dual language books in a variety of languages

Questioning: http://learningforward.org/docs/jsd-winter-2008/hill291.pdf?sfvrsn=2 (Hill & Flynn, 2008)

Using bilingual books: http://www.ohiorc.org/record/5187.aspx (Ernst-Slavit & Mulhern, 2003)

Translanguaging as a pedagogical tool: http://www.nysieb.ws.gc.cuny.edu/files/2012/06/FINAL-Translanguaging-Guide-With-Cover-1.pdf (Guide for Educators, Celic & Seltzer, 2011)

http://www.nysieb.ws.gc.cuny.edu/files/2014/12/Translanguaging-Guide-Curr-Inst-Final-December-2014.pdf (Guide for Educators, Hesson, Seltzer, & Woodley, 2014)

Cooperative learning and ELs: http://www.colorincolorado.org/article/cooperative-learning-strategies

Best practices for ELLs: http://ell.nwresd.org/node/74

REFERENCES

Abu El-Haj, T. R. (2006). *Elusive justice: Wrestling with difference and educational equity in everyday practice.* New York: Routledge.

August, D., & Shanahan, T. (Eds.). (2006). *Developing literacy in second-language learners. A report of the National Literacy Panel on Language-Minority Children and Youth.* Mahwah, NJ: Lawrence Erlbaum.

Beninghof, A., & Leensvaart, M. (2016). Co-teaching to support ELLs. *Educational Leadership, 70*–74.

Berg, H., Petrón, M., & Greybeck, B. (2012). Setting the foundation for working with English language learners in the secondary classroom. *American Secondary Education, 40*(3), 34–44.

Bernhard, J. K., Cummins, J., Campoy, F. A., Ada, A. F., Winsler, A., & Bleiker, C. (2006). Identity texts and literacy development among preschool English language learners: Enhancing learning opportunities for children at risk of learning disabilities. *Teachers College Record, 108,* 2380–2405.

Brisk, M. E. (2008). *Language, culture, and community in teacher education.* Mahwah, NJ: Lawrence Erlbaum (for the American Association of Colleges for Teacher Education).

Brisk, M. E. (2006). *Bilingual Education: From Compensatory to Quality Education.* Mahwah, NJ: Lawrence Erlbaum.

Brisk, M. E., Burgos, A., & Hamerla, S. (2004). *Situational context of education: A window into the world of bilingual learners.* Mahwah, NJ: Lawrence Erlbaum.

Brisk, M. E., & Harrington, M. M. (2000). *Literacy and bilingualism: A handbook for all teachers.* Mahwah, NJ: Lawrence Erlbaum.

Brooks, K., Adams, S. R., & Morita-Mullaney, T. (2010). Creating inclusive learning communities for students: Transforming school principals' perspectives. *Theory into Practice, 49,* 145–151.

Calderon, M., Slavin, R., & Sanchez, M. (2011). Effective instruction for English learners. *The Future of Children, 21*(1), 103–127.

Canagarajah, A. S. (2011). Translanguaging in the classroom: Emerging issues for research and pedagogy. *Applied Linguistics Review, 2,* 1–28.

Carrasquillo, A., & Rodriguez, J. (1998). Measuring success in bilingual education programs: Case studies of exemplary practices. *Reports-Evaluative,* 2–14.

Carrejo, D., Cortez, T., & Reinhartz, J. (2010). Exploring principal leadership roles within a community of practice to promote science performance of English language learners. *Academic Leadership, 8*(4).

Carroll, P. E., & Bailey, A. L. (2016). Do decision rules matter? A descriptive study of English language proficiency assessment classifications for English-language learners and native English speakers in fifth grade. *Language Testing, 33*(1), 23–52. doi:10.1177/0265532215576380.

Carter, T. P., & Chatfield, M. L. (1986). Effective bilingual schools: Implications for policy and practice. *American Journal of Education, 95* (l), 200–232.

Castañeda, M., Rodríguez-González, E., & Schulz, M. (2011). Enhancing reading proficiency in English language learners (ELLs): The importance of knowing your ELL in mainstream classrooms. *Tapestry Journal, 3*(1), 38–63.

Cazden, C. B. (1984). Effective instructional practices in bilingual education. [Research review commissioned by the National Institute of Education]. (ERIC Document Reproduction Service No. ED 249 768)

Celic, C., & Seltzer, K. (2011). Translanguaging: A CUNY-NYSIEB guide for educators. Retrieved May 25, 2016, at http://www.nysieb.ws.gc.cuny.edu/files/2012/06/FINAL-Translanguaging-Guide-With-Cover-1.pdf.

Choi, D. S., & Morrison, P. (2014). Learning to get it right: Understanding change processes in professional development for teachers of English learners. *Professional Development in Education, 40*(3), 416–435.

Coady, M., Hamann, E. T., Harrington, M., Pacheco, M., Pho, S., & Yedlin, J. (2008). Successful schooling for ELLs: Principles for building responsive learning environments. In L. S. Verplaetse & N. Migliacci (Eds.), *Inclusive pedagogy for English language learners: A handbook of research-informed practices* (pp. 245–255). New York: Lawrence Erlbaum.

Coleman, R., & Goldenberg, C. (2010). What does research say about effective practices for English learners? Part IV: Models for schools and districts. *Kappa Delta Pi Record, 46*(4), 156–163.

Craighead, E., & Ramanathan, H. (2007). Effective teacher interactions with English language learners in mainstream classes. *Research in the Schools, 14*(1), 60–71.

Creese, A., & Blackledge, A. (2010). Translanguaging in the bilingual classroom: A pedagogy for learning and teaching? *Modern Language Journal, 94*(1), 103–115.

Cummins, J., Bismilla, V., Chow, P., Cohen, S., Giampapa, F., Leoni, L., Sandhu, P., & Sastri, P. (2005). Affirming identity in multilingual classrooms. *Educational Leadership, 63*(1), 38–43.

Curtin, E. M. (2005). Teaching Practices for ESL Students. *Multicultural Education, 12*(3), 22–27.

de Jong, E. (2013). Preparing mainstream teachers for multilingual classrooms. *Association of Mexican-American Educators, 7*(2), 40–50.

de Jong, E. J. (2006). Integrated bilingual education: An alternative approach. *Bilingual Research Journal, 30*(1), 23–44.

de Jong, E. J. (2011). A review of "Towards multilingual education: Basque educational research from an international perspective." *Language & Education: An International Journal, 25*(1), 82–84. doi:10.1080/09500782.2010.494859.

de Jong, E. J., & Derrick-Mescua, M. (2003). Refining preservice teachers' questions for second language learners: Higher order thinking for all levels of language proficiency. *Sunshine State TESOL Journal 2*(2), 29–37.

de Jong, E. J., & Freeman, R. (2010). Bilingual approaches. In Leung, C., and Creese, A. (Eds.) *English as an additional language: Approaches to teaching linguistic minority students.* (pp. 108–122). London: SAGE.

de Jong, E. J., Gort, M., & Cobb, C. D. (2005). Bilingual education within the context of English-only policies: Three districts' responses to Question 2 in Massachusetts. *Educational Policy, 19*(4), 595–620.

de Jong, E. J., & Harper, C. A. (2005). Preparing mainstream teachers for English-language learners: Is being a good teacher good enough? *Teacher Education Quarterly, 32*(2), 101–124.

de Jong, E.J., & Lopez Estrada, P. (2011). The role of a teacher in structuring peer interaction. *Sunshine State TESOL Journal, 10* (1), 1–7.

de Oliveira, L. C., Gilmetdinova, A., & Pelaez Morales, C. (2015). The use of Spanish by a monolingual kindergarten teacher to support English language learners. *Language and Education, 29*(6), 1–21.

Deussen, T., Autio, E., Miller, B., Lockwood, A. T., & Stewart, V. (2008). *What teachers should know about instruction for English language learners: A report to Washington State.* Portland: NWREL.

Echevarria, J., Vogt, M. E., & Short, D. (2014). *Making content comprehensible for elementary English learners: The SIOP® model.* Second Edition. Boston: Allyn & Bacon.

Elfers, A. M., & Stritikus, T. (2013). How school and district leaders support classroom teachers' work with English language learners. *Educational Administration Quarterly, 20*(10), 1–40.

Ernst-Slavit, G., & Mulhern, M. (2003). Bilingual books: Promoting literacy and biliteracy in the second-language and mainstream classroom. *Reading Online*, 1–13.

Evans, B. A., & Hornberger, N. H. (2005). No child left behind: Repealing and "unpeeling" federal language education policy in the United States. *Language Policy, 4* (1), 87–106. http://dx.doi.org/10.1007/s10993-004-6566-2.

Ewald, J. (2005). Language-related episodes in an assessment context: A "small-group quiz." *The Canadian Modern Language Review, 61*(4), 565–586.

Freeman, Y., Freeman, D., & Mercuri, S. (2003). Helping middle and high school age English language learners achieve academic success. *NABE Journal of Research and Practice*, Winter, 110–122.

Galguera, T., & Hakuta, K. (1997). Linguistically diverse students. In H. J. Walberg & G. D. Haertel (Eds.), *Psychology and Educational Practice* (pp. 387–407). Berkeley, CA: McCutchan Publishers.

Gándara, P., & Hopkins, M. (Eds.). (2010). *Forbidden language: English learners and restrictive language policies.* New York: Teachers College Press.

Garbati, J. F., & Mady, C. J. (2015). Oral skill development in second languages: A review in search of best practices. *Theory & Practice in Language Studies, 5*(9), 1663–1770. doi:10.17507/tpls.0509.01.

Garcia, C., & Chun, H. (2016). Culturally responsive teaching and teacher expectations for Latino middle school students. *Journal of Latina/o Psychology*, doi:10.1037/lat0000061.

García, O. (2008). Teaching Spanish and Spanish in teaching in the U.S.: Integrating bilingual perspectives. In A. M. de Mejía and C. Helot (Eds.), *Integrated perspectives towards bilingual education: Bridging the gap between prestigious bilingualism and the bilingualism of minorities* (pp. 31–57). Clevedon, UK: Multilingual Matters.

García, O., & Yip, J. (2015). Introduction: Translanguaging: Practice briefs for educators. *Theory, Research and Action in Urban Education, 4*(1).

Gersten, R., & Baker, S. (2000). Practices for English language learners. *Special Education Programs*, 1–12.

Gersten, R., Baker, S. K., Shanahan, T., Linan-Thompson, S., Collins, P., & Scarcella, R. (2007). *Effective literacy and English language instruction for English learners in the elementary grades: A practice guide* (NCEE 2007-4011). Washington, DC: National Center for Education Evaluation and Regional Assistance, Institute of Education Sciences, U.S. Department of Education. Retrieved from http://ies.ed.gov/ncee.

Giambo, D., & Szecsi, T. (2015). Promoting and maintaining bilingualism and biliteracy: Cognitive and biliteracy benefits & strategies for monolingual teachers. *The Open Communication Journal*, 56–60. Retrieved September 2, 2015.

Gold. N. (2006). *Successful bilingual schools: Six effective programs in California.* San Diego: San Diego County Office of Education.

Gorski, P. C. (2013). *Reaching and teaching students in poverty.* New York: Teachers College Press.

Gort, M., de Jong, E. J., & Cobb, C. D. (2008). Seeing through a bilingual lens: Structural and ideological contexts of sheltered English immersion in three Massachusetts districts. *Journal of Educational Research and Policy Studies, 8*(2), 41–66.

Haneda, M., & Wells, G. (2012). Some key pedagogic principles for helping ELLs to succeed in school. *Theory into Practice, 51,* 297–304.

Hesson, S., Seltzer, K., & Woodley, H. H. (2014). *Translanguaging in curriculum & instruction: A CUNY-NYSEIB guide for educators.* New York: CUNY-NYSIEB.

Hill, J., & Flynn, K. (2008). Asking the right question. *National Staff Development Council, 29* (1), 46–52.

Honigsfeld, A., & Dove, M. G. (2010). *Collaboration and co-teaching. Strategies for English learners.* Thousand Oaks, CA: Corwin Press.

Hornberger, N. H. (2002). Multilingual language policies and the continua of biliteracy: An ecological approach. *Language Policy, 1*(1), 27–51.

Hornberger, N. H., & Ricento, T. (1996). Language planning and policy and the ELT profession. *Special topic issue, TESOL Quarterly, 30*(3), 401–427.

Horwitz, A. R., Uro, G., Price-Baugh, R., Simon, C., Uzzell, R., Lewis, S., & Casserly, M. (2009). *Succeeding with English language learners: Lessons learned from the great city schools.* The Council of the Great City Schools.

Islam, C., & Park, M. (2015). Preparing teachers to promote culturally relevant teaching: Helping English language learners in the classroom. *Multicultural Education,* 39–43.

Kopriva, R. J., Emick, J. E., Hipolito-Delgado, C. P., & Cameron, C. A. (2007). Do proper accommodation assignments make a difference? Examining the impact of improved decision making on scores for English language learners. *Educational Measurement: Issues & Practice, 26*(3), 11–20. doi:10.1111/j.1745-3992.2007.00097.x.

Kumashiro, K. (2004). *Against common sense: Teaching and learning toward social justice.* New York: Routledge Falmer.

Li, J. (2012). Principles of effective English language learners' pedagogy. *Research in Review, 3,* 1–20.

López, F., & Iribarren, J. (2014). Creating and sustaining inclusive instructional settings for English language learners: Why, what, and how. *Theory into Practice, 53,* 106–114.

Lucas, T., & Villegas, A. M. (2013). Preparing linguistically responsive teachers: Laying the foundation in preservice teacher education, *Theory into Practice, 52*(2), 98–109.

Lucero, A. (2014). Teachers' use of linguistic scaffolding to support the academic language development of first-grade emergent bilingual students. *Journal of Early Childhood Literacy, 14*(4), 534–561. doi:10.1177/1468798413512848.

Lyster, R. (2004). Differential effects of prompts and recasts in form-focused instruction. *Studies in Second Language Acquisition, 26,* 399–432.

Mace-Matluck, B. J. (1990). The effective schools movement: Implications for Title VII and Bilingual Education Projects. *Annual Conference Journal NABE '88–89* (pp. 83–95). Washington, DC: NABE.

McGee, A., Haworth, P., & Macintyre, L. (2015). Leadership practices to support teaching and learning for English language learners. *TESOL Quarterly, 49*(1), 92–114.

Mohan, B. (1990). *LEP students and the integration of language and content: Knowledge structures and tasks.* Washington, DC: Proceedings of the First Research Symposium on Limited English Proficient Student Issues.

Noddings, N. (1984). *Caring: A feminine approach to ethics and moral education.* Berkeley, CA: University of California Press.

Nzai, V. E., Gomez, P., Reyna, C., & Jen, K. (2012). Non-native English speaking elementary ELL teachers' culturally responsive leadership profile in an ESL context. *Colombian Applied Linguistics, 14*(1), 88–108.

Office of English Language Acquisition (OELA). (2015). Profiles of English learners (ELs). (Fast Facts). Washington, DC: U.S. Department of Education. Retrieved from http://www2.ed.gov/about/offices/list/oela/fast-facts/pel.pdf.

Olsen, B., & and Kirtman, L. (2002). Teacher as mediator of school reform: An examination of teacher practice in 36 California restructuring schools. *Teachers College Record, 104*(2). 301–324.

Ovando, C. J. (2003). Bilingual education in the United States: Historical development and current issues. *Bilingual Research Journal, 27*(1), 1–24.

Pacific Policy Research Center. (2010). *Successful bilingual and immersion education models/programs*. Honolulu: Kamehameha Schools, Research & Evaluation Division.

Palmer, B. C., Chen, C., & Chang, S. (2006). The impact of biculturalism on language and literacy Development: Teaching Chinese English language learners. *Reading Horizons, 46*(4), 239–265.

Pease-Alvarez, L., Garcia, E. E., & Espinosa, P. (1991). Effective instruction for language-minority students: An early childhood case study. *Early Childhood Research Quarterly, 6*, 347–361.

Purdy, J. (2008). Inviting conversation: Meaningful talk about texts for English language learners. *Literacy, 42*(1), 44–51. doi:10.1111/j.1467-9345.2008.00479.x.

Ragan, A., & Lesaux, N. (2006). Federal, state, and district level English language learner program entry and exit requirements: Effects on the education of language minority learners. *Education Policy Analysis Archives, 14*(20). Retrieved from: http://epaa.asu.edu/epaa/v14n20/.

Razfar, A. A. (2012). ¡Vamos a jugar counters! Learning mathematics through funds of knowledge, play, and the third space. *Bilingual Research Journal, 35*(1), 53–75. doi:10.1080/15235882.2012.668868.

Reed, B., & Railsback, J. (2003). Strategies and resources for mainstream teachers of English language learners. *Northwest Regional Educational Laboratory*, 1–43.

Reyes, A., & Garcia, A. (2014). Turnaround policy and practice: A case study of turning around a failing school with English-language-learners. *Urban Revision, 46*, 349–371.

Ricento, T. K., & Hornberger, N. H. (1996). Unpeeling the onion: Language planning and policy and the ELT professional. *TESOL Quarterly, 30*(3), 401–428.

Rodríguez, C. C., Filler, J., & Higgins, K. (2012). Using primary language support via computer to improve reading comprehension skills of first-grade English language learners. *Computers in The Schools, 29*(3), 253–267. doi:10.1080/07380569.2012.702718.

Ruiz, R. (1984). Orientations in language planning. *NABE Journal, 8*, 15–34.

Scanlan, M., & Palmer, D. (2009). Race, power, and (in)equity within two-way immersion settings. *Urban Review, 41*(5), 391–415.

Stritikus, T. (2002). *Immigrant children and the politics of English-only: Views from the classroom*. New York: LFB Scholarly Publishing LLC.

Thompson, L. W. (2004). *Literacy development for English language learners: Classroom challenges in the NCLB age*. Monterey, CA: CTB/McGraw Hill.

Tikunoff, W. J., & Vazquez-Faria, J. A. (1982). Successful instruction for bilingual schooling. *Peabody Journal of Education, 59*(4), 234–271.

Torres-Guzmán, M. E., & Goodwin, A. L. (1995). Urban bilingual teachers and mentoring for the future. *Education and Urban Society, 28*, 48–66.

Valenzuela, A. (1999). *Subtractive schooling: US-Mexican youth and the politics of caring*. Albany: State University of New York Press.
Wiese, A., & García, E. E. (1998). The Bilingual Education Act: Language minority students and equal educational opportunity. *Bilingual Research Journal, 22*(1), 1–18.
Zwiers, J. (2007). *Building academic language: Essential practices for content classrooms*. San Francisco: Jossey-Bass.

Chapter Two

Planning Instruction for ELs

Culture, Language, and the Curriculum

Mayra C. Daniel

The influences of culture and language development on English learners' academic success cannot be overlooked. The author addresses factors that teachers must consider in curriculum planning if they wish to situate students and teachers as co-learners and collaborators invested in creating an efficient multilingual schoolhouse.

In this conversation, the author begins with a look at how second language development is shaped by English learners' (ELs) need to master the target language of study, the cultural mismatch these students may experience at school, and how these processes influence classroom instruction. She offers ideas of how teachers might examine learners' use of their linguistic and cultural repertoires (García & Wei, 2014) in lesson planning and curricular development.

Teachers must ensure the curriculum equitably covers ELs' needs to learn English and master disciplinary content (Daniel, 2016) while addressing the Common Core State Standards (CCSS) (Valdés, Menken, & Castro, 2015). In this chapter, the author offers suggestions for the classroom centered on ensuring social justice is a focus of instruction across the content areas (Daniel, 2016) and is based on understandings of second language acquisition processes (Bialystok, 2011).

SCHOOLING AND CULTURAL INFLUENCES

Across the world, educators are in a new era of teaching and learning due to the ways technology allows communication across continents in real time. In the schoolhouse, this means that it is commonplace for students to interact using multimodal inputs and outputs simultaneously. It is also natural for learners to daily use all the languages that they know, in and out of the classroom, at whatever level of proficiency they have reached.

Languages are evolving more quickly than ever before. The influences of popular culture and the on the spot communications facilitated by current technologies through the worldwide-web allow communications that are not delimited by distance or time zones. In our schools today, there is also the side benefit of the increasingly diverse student demographic and its contribution to intercultural communication.

As an educator interested in ensuring that all ELs master content while in the process of developing English, you are probably finding that students in 2017 learn differently from those in the past and may more efficiently examine how they learn with the help of current technologies. Keep in mind that research suggests students develop language more quickly while using multimodal avenues within curricular models that acknowledge their cultural capital and academic histories.

Collier and Thomas's (2014) research into dual language programs supports a multiliteracies and bilingual approach. Their suggestions for planning curricula help us understand that the linguistic *balance* achieved in dual language programs is "a culturally-responsive approach" that is based on "culturally-relevant curriculum and instruction" (p. 3). As a teacher, you will want to examine cultural and linguistic influences on learning and what this implies for lesson planning and learners' long-term academic achievement.

Interpersonal Communications: Cultural Mismatch

Educators know that language arises from human beings' need to communicate and to make sense of their world. ELs develop language when they have a need to do so—in order to make friends and learn what their teachers require of them at school. Along with learning everyday English, ELs are acquiring academic discourses across disciplinary boundaries. Current technologies enhance how culture contributes to and shapes students' multiliteracies in and outside the school community (Daniel & Shin, 2015). "A multiliteracies perspective transforms the schoolhouse into an environment that embraces questioning and learning through critical pedagogy (Daniel & Huizenga-McCoy, 2014, p. 182).

The schoolhouse presents an unfamiliar cultural environment for ELs, not only in the classroom but also in the principal's office, and even in the food selections available at the cafeteria. The ELs are immersed in an English-speaking world that may not seem welcoming to them. They experience cultural mismatch when they do not understand all the nuances related to how they see others communicating. They may perceive that their sense of self and their identity does not align with the community's expectations.

Teachers cannot assume that all is well as ELs develop English and their bicultural identities begin to form. Students' perception of their place in their new society may still seem uncertain to them long after arrival in the adopted country. They may continue to struggle in interpersonal communications if they do not understand the verbal and nonverbal forms of expressions they encounter. Thus, teachers need to plan culturally relevant curricula that address challenges in second language acquisition and validates all learners' identities (Daniel, 2016).

Disciplinary Literacy

Language is intertwined with disciplinary literacy and the forms of expressions and voice used to share knowledge in each discipline. When ELs first enroll in U.S. classrooms, their workload is greater than that of the monolingual, English-speaking native. ELs working to master English may not have the language to ask questions about what they are learning or what they are being asked to do.

In physics class, for example, students might use the language of mathematics as the conceptual vehicle to access, understand, and share information that explains scientific phenomena. ELs reporting observations in writing after conducting a science experiment need to know how to write sentences that fit this purpose.

Similarly, in the social studies classroom, students will successfully compare and contrast two governmental systems with the appropriate teacher guidance that focuses on the language the ELs need to complete the task. When teachers model for students how to write for different purposes, the ELs will more easily understand texts written for the different disciplines and develop the literacy needed to share the knowledge they are mastering in writing formats (Brisk, 2015).

CONSIDERATIONS IN IMPLEMENTING STANDARDS-BASED CURRICULA

Planning curricula for ELs requires that teachers' pedagogy encompass more than disciplinary expertise and also include the ability to teach language. Exploring learners' schooling and nonschooling experiences prior to their families' immigration to the United States is key to identifying students' curricular needs. Because ELs represent numerous cultural backgrounds, experiences, and languages, it is impossible to make assumptions about their academic needs. For many, English is a second, third, or fourth language.

As you plan lessons while consulting the CCSS (Valdés, Menken, & Castro, 2015), you will need to become familiar with the backgrounds of your student populations to identify their individual educational needs. The CCSS are a guiding instrument, but they are devoid of the personal information that will allow you to link your instructional tasks to your students' cultural capital. In addition, examine your own cultural norms and expectations. As you explore your philosophical stances, you will develop more accepting perspectives of what you may not have experienced and may not fully understand from your own life. This is key in your work with ELs.

Plurilingual[1] speakers in the United States are developing English using the knowledge base they developed in multilingual environments—in their communities of residence prior to and during their trajectory to the United States. Many ELs were born in border communities where several languages were part of their daily interactions. Some lived in refugee camps in more than one nation while in transit to their final destination. Others are heritage language speakers (ELs born in the United States) growing up in multilingual environments.

ELs' diverse experiences represent their unique linguistic and cultural expertise. It demands teachers be cultural mediators in the classroom, in the playground, and within their school communities. It is as important to teach academic content as it is to make certain that classroom environments embody philosophies of equity and social justice paradigms that concretely link the schoolhouse to the community of the learners and their families (Daniel, 2016).

García and Wei (2014) tell us that these learners, whom they label emergent bilinguals (EBs), are developing languages using their entire linguistic repertoire. When learners are placed in an English as a second language class, their prior knowledge helps them access all pathways available to create meaning (Bialystok, 2011).

Teachers must investigate students' languages and cultures to better understand their cultural capital and support their academic achievement using culturally relevant pedagogy (Daniel, 2016). Teachers familiar with their students' communities will plan instruction that is culturally responsive and ensures social justice is a natural and integral part of the classroom curriculum.

What teachers do in their classroom has to link in some way to students' funds of knowledge (González, Moll, & Amanti, 2005). The identity of all learners, whether or not they are monolingual or plurilingual, is shaped within their communities as they learn to interact efficiently and appropriately in different contexts.

Limitations of the CCSS

Adoption of the CCSS has raised educators' awareness of what students need to know to succeed in the world. However, the standards fail to address the challenges that teachers encounter when attempting to plan lessons that meet the CCSS while also teaching English and discipline-specific academic language to ELs. Today's educators are faced with the task of implementing standards written for monolingual students that do not directly make any recommendations for ELs.

Massey (2015) considers that CCSS do not make suggestions to teachers for planning instruction for students who are first- and second-generation immigrants. He is concerned with children from Mexican backgrounds who will begin their schooling "with limited English ability and limited exposure to the kinds of knowledge and information that are typical in middle class . . . families" (p. 10).

Similarly, Wiley (2015) is concerned that the CCSS may perpetuate a deficiency model that does not acknowledge the linguistic capital of students' communities and families. He recommends educators "scrutinize the extent to which the ELA CCSS reflect the needs and specific linguistic and cultural resources of all students" (p. 11). Nieto (2015) uses the word *silence* to describe how the CCSS fail to acknowledge ELs' educational needs.

Offering a different and more positive point of view are Brisk and Proctor (2015). They suggest educators interpret the CCSS as a vehicle to implement high quality bilingual programs. Their argument is that the CCSS will serve astute teachers to demonstrate that students:

1. will benefit from discipline-specific content instruction in the language in which they are most proficient,
2. will find it easier to formulate and share their ideas in bilingual environments, and
3. can meet the CCSS in schooling paradigms that support balanced bilingualism and biliteracy.

Wong Fillmore and Martinez (2015) guide us further to use the CCSS to raise ELs' academic achievement. They tell us that meeting the linguistic demands of the CCSS requires teachers support ELs to develop higher literacy levels, especially while they are in the process of acquiring English.

Engaging ELs means the curriculum must meet their plurilingual language needs. Curricular materials cannot overly simplify language or decrease the level of the disciplinary content. Educators strive for ELs to be so interested in what they are learning that they will be incentivized to trudge through those moments when they struggle to comprehend. Multimodal instruction, and especially instruction supported by current technologies, considers students' multiple intelligences and gives them opportunities to experiment with language.

As educators, the message that we must hold in our hearts is the belief that in U.S. classrooms, teachers are free to teach in ways that support students' dynamic bilingualism (García & Flores, 2013). If we believe this, our work will ensure equitable rather than deficit educational models in our schools.

PREPARING TO EXPLORE LEARNERS' COMMUNITIES

As teachers ask questions about students' educational needs, they look for the answers directly from the learners, their families, and communities. Educators must all be ethnographers who observe and engage members of the school community in conversations that will inform them about the lives of their students.

An important part of your work as a teacher is to recognize the knowledge that students bring to school and use this to plan culturally relevant instruction. In your first step, explore the words that you will select to refer to your students. You want to identify but not rank and label students. The U.S. federal government refers to ELs as *limited English proficient* students

(LEPs). This term points to students' lack of English-language proficiency, and does not identify what they know.

While the more accepted acronym used to refer to nonnative speakers of English is ELs, García (2015) proposes using the descriptor *emergent bilinguals* (EBs) as a better choice. She argues that this term is "full of future and promise" and that it identifies "bilingualism as an important goal and aspiration" that "moves us forward from the conversations we have had in the past" and, most importantly, demonstrates "an emergence of new understanding about language and bilingualism" (p. 23).

Your second step is to engage in ethnographic work that will provide you concrete ideas for planning culturally relevant lessons. Make time to learn about the neighborhood of your school and make home visits to your students' families.

In one of her graduate-level courses, the author asks teachers to design a lesson after conducting a funds of knowledge project (González, Moll, & Amanti, 2005). The teachers write open-ended questions as they prepare to conduct an interview with an EL's family. They use the information they gain in the conversation to paint a picture of the family's goals for their children.

Interview questions facilitate an exploration of the parents' educational and immigrant experiences, their understandings of schooling in the United States, and what they perceive should be their involvement in the school. The resulting lesson plan includes components that focus on identification of the learner's cultural capital and demands reflection to identify ways to include these in the lesson:

Part I. A description of the student and the parents or caregivers, including:

- Student's age and educational background
- Parents' educational background
- Description of neighborhood where the family resides
- Educational goals of parents and children
- Observed home literacy

Part II. School information:

- Description of school and academic program for ELs
- Demographic information (use school report card)

Part III. Name of lesson plan that includes:

- Clearly replicable content and language objectives
- What student will be able to do (using active verbs such as count, describe, prepare, demonstrate)

Part IV. Rationale for lesson based on a reflection of the home visit:

- Anticipatory set
- Procedures
- Student's strengths and weaknesses
- Student's special needs due to EL status and attendance constraints
- Approaches to reading for student *appropriate with grade*
- Curricular modifications / translanguaging approaches
- Description of materials to be used in the lesson
- Recommendations for colleagues who teach the student in content areas classes that focus on literacy across the curriculum
- Identification of student's funds of family knowledge
- Suggestions for promoting links between home and school
- Assessment plan

After conducting the home visit, the teachers report that their eyes are open to what is not possible to uncover in a parent-teacher conference. While many experience some uncertainty in preparing to conduct the interview, they are always happy to have been made to engage the family in the conversation.

On their return to the graduate class, many teachers report having felt they were welcomed and treated as an important guest in their student's home. Often, during or after the visit, the teachers receive an invitation to a meal or a family celebration. The visit facilitates respectful partnerships.

Many teachers participate in a home visit that lasts much longer then they anticipated, yet they find the time beneficial. The teachers report that during the visit they learned that there is much they can do to reach out to involve families. A key piece of the visit is the sharing with the guardians or parents that in the United States, parents are welcome to be partners with their children's teachers because their voices count.

Chapter Two

ACTIVE OUTREACH TO DIVERSE COMMUNITIES: TAKING ACTION

Parents who have not attended U.S. schools will need help identifying schooling expectations for their children. It is imperative that they feel safe turning to their children's teachers for help. Immigrant parents may not know what composes sanctioned schooling behavior in the United States nor what the leadership structures demand of the teacher and the student.

Han (2012) emphasizes advocacy based on teachers' evolving knowledge base of immigrant families' challenges. She divides parental stages of adaptation to U.S. culture into four areas: *cultural survivors, cultural learners, cultural connectors, and cultural leaders*. Educators' task is to identify where families may be in these stages and to find ways to provide them the support they need. Within budgetary limits the schoolhouse must support immigrant families as they work to integrate their cultural beliefs with those of mainstream U.S. society.

According to Han (2012), pathways to becoming a cultural leader take time. The *cultural survivor* who is concerned with putting food on the table has little time for anything other than work. The *cultural learner* is the person ready to begin to learn what schooling in the United States is about. The *cultural connector* has gained the expertise to guide others new to the system. Lastly, the *cultural leader* is the individual at the highest level of cultural adaptation.

The person who has reached the stage of being a *cultural leader* is acknowledged to lead the cultural community. The leader has the knowledge of the new culture and the expertise to navigate the miasma of what may at first appear to negate the rights of the nonnative English speaker. Our goal as educators should be that in every family of ELs there be a member at the level of being labeled the cultural leader and that we be there to offer our support to those at the first three stages of adaptation.

In a highly diverse school district, five bilingual teachers and the author reached out to parents of ELs. The group of educators organized after school meetings that combined sharing supper with the families, babysitting by college-student teacher candidates, and presentations by bilingual classroom teachers that covered topics from the U.S. school system to how parents can help their children with homework. Not only were sessions well attended but parents demonstrated an interest in continuing the conversations after the evenings of the meetings. The group observed that advocacy that is genuine is key to parental involvement.

In schools across the nation, teachers and school administrators can evaluate the quality and effectiveness of their district's outreach efforts by asking themselves the following questions:

1. What do we do to show that we value parental input?
2. How do we encourage families to participate in school activities?
3. Are we creating opportunities for all parents to participate?
4. What do we do for the parents who work after school and cannot attend meetings?
5. How do we communicate with parents if we lack translators for their languages?
6. Whose leadership do we applaud? Who leads the school's parent organization?

Academic Achievement and Second Language Acquisition Processes

A reconceptualization of the relationship between ELs' success at school and how educators understand second language acquisition processes (SLA) is changing teachers' practices. Let's begin by recognizing Canagarajah's (2013) definition of *translingual competence*. He defines this as the learners' ability to acquire form and simultaneously develop the expertise to use language in different sociocultural contexts. He proposes that language acquisition learners add to their existing linguistic repertoires as their identities adapt to the circumstances in which they find themselves.

It is essential to recognize that the sociocultural context's contribution to language and cognitive development and the learner's level of intercultural competence (Kramsch, 2014; Wiley & Rolstad, 2014) are key contributors to SLA. We will now examine SLA within the premise that new views of how human beings acquire additional languages are providing educators wider lenses for instructional planning. We will base this exploration on Collier and Thomas's long-term research (2014) suggesting that the pedagogy used in dual language (DL) programs leads ELs to higher levels of academic achievement and is more cost-effective than remedial programs.

DL pedagogy is a bilingual instruction model that aims for learners to develop intercultural and multilingual competence. In this model teachers use authentic high quality materials rather than translated texts. Learning in

DL programs does not separate languages into distinct silos of knowledge that are accessed separately, but instead acknowledges a back and forth transference of information across all the learners' languages.

In the DL model, students are recognized to learn best when instruction begins using the language they understand best and then continues to be used to build linguistic capacity in the other language. Even if you do not know your students' home language(s), you can encourage them to use this language as they work to understand instruction delivered in English. Students will learn using materials written in different languages within a single classroom. On their own, or while working in small groups, students can write and illustrate multilingual texts, which they will take home and share with family members.

Effective bilingual education recognizes that SLA is neither a linear nor a predictable process. It is not governed by the teaching of language as discrete skills in a predetermined order. It is key to accept that while standards are helpful in setting curricular goals, ELs may progress through stages of SLA at different rates. Indeed, often students appear to bypass stages in SLA that many years ago were thought to be prerequisites to higher levels. In the classroom, your focus should be to help the learners comprehend.

Always teach language in context and provide students ongoing opportunities to examine how they are learning and to share their knowledge with their classmates. Teach students to identify important ideas and to use the new language they are encountering in their texts. Help them to monitor their comprehension and include moments in lessons to check for understanding. When you require the students to complete activities such as think-pair-share, you are evaluating them, plus showing them how to monitor their understanding.

Bialystok's research (2011) provides suggestions for teachers to plan lessons because her work helps our understandings of SLA. We now know that multilingual learners do not use only one language or one part of the brain as they learn. The executive control system of the brain always selects from its "competing options" (Bialystok, 2011, p. 229). This system, the decision-making part of the brain, decides what incoming language input will be selected after initial processing occurs throughout the entire system. The bilingual brain works as one entity that seamlessly works to complete all tasks using information from all the languages it has stored to produce language (Grosjean, 2008).

The aforementioned researchers' work suggests to us that a multilingual learner is at an advantage in the classroom in that he or she has more pathways to understand language and complete classroom tasks while using the whole brain to process language. Therefore, we might assume two concepts are true. First, the ELs work harder as they sift through all the input that they receive. Secondly, because the ELs have more information to help them understand, their executive control leads them to deeper levels of comprehension, interpretation, and meaning-making.

The task for teachers is to support students' dynamic bilingualism and teach them the language they need to express their ideas at school as they translanguage to comprehend. Instruction must be based on the idea that all learners want to learn and will do so if given the freedom to grow at their own pace while receiving support and appropriate modeling from their teachers.

CONCLUSIONS AND RECOMMENDATIONS FOR THE CLASSROOM

If teachers hold the philosophy that language development is " always emergent, continuous, never ending, and shaped by relationships with people, texts, and situations" (García & Wei, 2014, p. 125), they will create opportunities for students to learn in safe plurilingual spaces. In your work:

1. *Help students work to express themselves orally and in writing.* Teach them to use graphic organizers (GOs) to organize their ideas and summarize key points before composing. Use the GOs as stepping-stones from which the students will experiment with new modes of expression. Students will struggle to identify supporting evidence for arguments, and GOs help them to identify these and create strong arguments.
2. *Engage students in assignments that provide opportunities to develop expertise, using different types of language for different purposes.* Ask the ELs to describe, persuade, argue, inform, or support an idea or a position, and to do so in different contexts: formal and informal social situations, political and/or academic environments.
3. *Acknowledge that ELs will need visual input to share their ideas as they are developing their English-language proficiency.* Use nontraditional types of homework tasks such as PowerPoint presentations as

scaffolds to compose written narratives and to support the ELs who are working hard to remember both the content they want to share and the right form to use. Use current technologies to create links between in and out of school learning and to add multimodal avenues to learning tasks.
4. *Share mentor texts with students.* Work with them to deconstruct the writing. They will see the effort the author put into identifying key ideas, stating these clearly, and justifying them comprehensibly. Your students will be encouraged when they grasp the efforts that all authors put into their writing. Mentor texts also provide concrete examples of writing at the level expected to meet the CCSS.
5. *Give students opportunities to explore language in the classroom at the moment they have questions.* ELs love to compare and contrast expressions across their languages. Offer minilessons when students' questions demonstrate they are intrigued with language forms. When your classroom is a safe place to translanguage, your students will see that comprehension is the goal of schooling and communication.
6. *Create moments to develop new interpretations.* Keep in mind that in conversations, human beings create new interpretations and understandings as they share their ideas, hear what others say, and interpret their commitment and justification (Daniel, 2010). Use safe spaces in social media applications to provide the students a medium for collaboration and communication (Davis, 2014).

Technology Resources

- Organize biliteracy centers that incorporate the use of technology to focus on developing the four language modalities (Mercuri & Ramos, 2015). Storybird (1.1.2) will help students develop their writing. Poster with Glogster EDU (2016) focuses on the development of writing skills through reading.
- With the online presentation software program PowToon (1.1.1), students can create animated movies or presentations for science or social studies class.
- Use the interactive media tool Thinglink (2015) to give your students links to photos and videos that will address comprehension of both content and language.

- Research available free applications that address students' vocabulary and reading comprehension needs on this website: http://www.readingrockets.org/teaching/reading101/literacyapps/.
- Kidblog allows students to participate in academic discussions in a safe blogging community; http://kidblog.org/home/.
- Using Fakebook students can chart information about books: plot, characters, events, interpersonal relationships; http://www.classtools.net/FB/home-page.

NOTE

1. A plurilingual speaker is defined in this chapter as an individual who effectively negotiates communications in one to several languages. Plurilinguals may not possess high levels of literacy in all the languages that they use to transact meaning and/or engage in interpersonal communications. For these individuals, the languages they use to communicate serve many purposes and are a source of pride because they enhance the person's communicative competence.

REFERENCES

Bialystok, E. (2011). Reshaping the mind: The benefits of bilingualism. *Canadian Journal of Experimental Psychology, 65*(4), 229–235.

Brisk, M. E. (2015). *Engaging students in academic literacies: Genre-based pedagogy for K–5 classrooms.* New York: Routledge.

Brisk, M. E., & Proctor, C. P. (2015). What do the Common Core State Standards mean for bilingual education? In G. Valdés, K. Menken, & M. Castro (Eds.), *Common core bilingual and English language learners* (pp. 15–16). Philadelphia, PA: Caslon Publishing.

Canagarajah, S. (2013). *Translingual practice: Global Englishes and cosmopolitan relations.* Abingdon, UK: Routledge.

Collier, V. P., & Thomas, W. P. (2014). *Creating dual language schools for a transformed world: Administrators' speak.* Albuquerque, NM: Fuentes Press.

Daniel, M. (2016). Critical pedagogy's power in English language teaching. In L. R. Jacobs & C. Hastings (Eds.), *The importance of social justice in English language teaching* (pp. 25–38). Alexandria, VA: TESOL Press.

Daniel, M. C. (2010). La Preparación del maestro: Una examinación de las voces de los capacitadores que enseñan en las escuelas normales de Guatemala. *Education and Learning Research Journal, GIST, 4*(1), 127–137.

Daniel, M. C., & Huizenga-McCoy, M. (2014). Art as a medium for bilingualism and biliteracy: Suggestions from the research literature. *GIST Education and Learning Journal, 8,* 177–188.

Daniel, M. C., & Shin, D-S. (2015). Exploring new paths to academic literacy for English learners. *The Tapestry Journal (6)*1, 1–10.

Davis, V. (2014). A guidebook for social media in the classroom. Retrieved February 11, 2016, from http://www.edutopia.org/blog/guidebook-social-media-in-classroom-vicki-davis.

García, O. (2015). How should we refer to students who are acquiring English as an additional language? In G. Valdés, K. Menken, & M. Castro (Eds.), *Common core bilingual and English language learners* (pp. 23–24). Philadelphia, PA: Caslon Publishing.

García, O., & Flores, N. (2013). Multilingualism and Common Core State Standards in the U.S. In S. May (Ed.), *The multilingual turn: Implications for SLA, TESOL, and bilingual education*. New York: Routledge.

García, O., & Wei, L. (2014). *Translanguaging: Language, bilingualism, and education*. London, England: Palgrave Macmillan.

Glogster EDU (2016). Boston, MA: Glogster EC Inc.

González, N., Moll, L., and Amanti, C. (Eds.). (2005). *Funds of knowledge for teaching in Latino households*. Mahwah, NJ: Lawrence Erlbaum.

Grosjean, F. (2008). *Studying bilinguals*. New York: Oxford University Press.

Han, Y. C. (2012). From survivors to leaders: Stages of immigrant parents involvement. In E. G. Kugler (Ed.), *Innovative voices in education: Engaging diverse communities* (pp. 171–186). Lanham, MD: Rowman & Littlefield.

Kramsch, C. (2014). Teaching foreign languages in an era of globalization: An introduction. *The Modern Language Journal, 98*(1), 296–311.

Massey, D. S. (2015). Who will the Common Core State Standards serve? How do they reflect 21st century demographic realities? In G. Valdés, K. Menken, & M. Castro (Eds.), *Common core bilingual and English language learners* (pp. 9–10). Philadelphia, PA: Caslon Publishing.

Mercuri, S., & Ramos, L. (2015). Technology-based biliteracy centers for the 21st-century learner. *GIST Education and Learning Research Journal, 9*, 196–216.

Nieto, D. (2015). How are students designated as English language learners represented in the Common Core State Standards? In G. Valdés, K. Menken, & M. Castro (Eds.), *Common core bilingual and English language learners* (pp. 13–14). Philadelphia, PA: Caslon Publishing.

PowToon (Version 1.1.1) [Online Software]. London, UK: PowToon Limited.

Storybird (Version 1.1.2) [Online software]. Storybird, Inc.

Thinglink (2015) [Online Software]. Thinglink.

Valdés, G., Menken, K., & Castro, M. (2015). *Common core bilingual and English language learners*. Philadelphia, PA: Caslon Publishing.

Wiley, T. G. (2015). In what ways are the Common Core State Standards de facto language education policy? In G. Valdés, K. Menken, & M. Castro (Eds.), *Common core bilingual and English language learners* (pp. 10–11). Philadelphia, PA: Caslon Publishing.

Wiley, T.G., & Rolstad, K. (2014). The Common Core State Standards and the great divide. *International Multilingual Research Journal, 8*, 1–18.

Wong Fillmore, L., & Martinez, R. B. (2015). Content are language demands. In G. Valdés, K. Menken, & M. Castro (Eds.), *Common core bilingual and English language learners* (pp. 155–161). Philadelphia, PA: Caslon Publishing.

Chapter Three

Developing Bilingualism and Biliteracy in Content Instruction Using a Linguistic Integrative Perspective

Aida A. Nevárez-La Torre

Identification of effective pedagogical practices used to teach language, literacy, and content in bilingual classrooms is a topic of interest for today's classroom teachers. This discussion explores teachers' practices based on evidence-based pedagogy that effectively supports an integrative language perspective in developing bilingualism and biliteracy.

Beyond acquiring oracy in more than one language, learners who possess the knowledge and skill to read and write in more than one language are considered *biliterate* (literacy in two languages) or *multiliterate* (literacy in more than two languages). These constructs are complex in nature and point to multidimensional interrelationships between multilingualism (de Jong, 2011) and literacy in teaching and learning.

Although research in the field of literacy in one language (monoliteracy) has been very prolific, there is a dearth of explorations that focus on reading and writing in two or more languages (Escamilla et al., 2014; Moll, Sáez, & Dworin, 2001). Historically accepted notions of bilingualism and biliteracy have favored teaching language and reading in one language separate from the other language. However, during the past two decades, there has been a gradual evolution in our understanding of the requirements of reading and writing in two or more languages.

Escamilla and colleagues (2014), García (2009), Oller (2005), and Sebba (2012) argue for integrative views of language that support multilingual reading. Specifically, they advocate for instruction where: (a) languages network with one another; (b) skills and strategies interact dynamically across languages; (c) the rich linguistic repertoire of bilingual students is used to negotiate and transact meaning with authentic bilingual and multimodal texts, and (d) the reading process and performance of bilingual readers are compared to those of other bilingual readers.

In this chapter, the author describes the practices used by six bilingual teachers to teach academic content of social studies and Spanish language arts in three dual language bilingual charter schools. The discussion focuses on the ways their linguistic integrative practices mirror evidence-based pedagogy recommended in the scholarly literature to develop bilingualism and biliteracy.

CHANGING VIEWS OF BILINGUALISM AND BILITERACY

A fractional view of bilingualism sees a bilingual as two monolinguals in one person (Grosjean, 2008). Similarly, a monolingual view of biliteracy emphasizes the separation of languages, imposes a view of reading, which dichotomizes communication into disconnected spheres. For instance, reading in Spanish involves the development of vocabulary, decoding, fluency, and comprehension skills disconnected from those skills used when reading in English.

This view is based on a position that stipulates "that even young bilinguals have a two-language system with two lexicons in the mind, each operating independently of the other" (Pearson, Fernández, & Oller, 1995, p. 348). Cummins (2005) adds that this perspective requires a strict separation of languages in instruction within bilingual programs (p. 2).

Currently, the view of monolingual reading as imposed on multilingual learners is seen as restrictive. It has been argued that this view does not acknowledge the sophisticated knowledge of language held by bilinguals, or their creativity of using language to communicate (Cenoz & Gorter, 2011).

Cummins has reasoned that this view fails to acknowledge a common underlying linguistic proficiency across languages, which may support the transfer of cognitive/academic or literacy-related proficiencies from one language to another (1979, p. 232). Additionally, it does not represent a realistic and authentic picture of what vocabulary knowledge is really like for multilingual readers (Grosjean, 2008; Mancilla-Martínez, Pan, & Vagh, 2011;

Pearson & Fernández, 1994; Poulin-Dubois, Bialystok, Blaye, Polonia, & Yott, 2012).

In recent decades, scholarly discussions have documented changes in understanding the requirements of reading and writing in two or more languages. The term *multiliteracies* acknowledges that literacy teaching in the 21st century should be more responsive to the diversity of cultures and the variety of languages within societies (New London Group, 1996). In other words, contemporary conceptualizations of literacy take into account the cultural diversity of contexts and the resourceful linguistic repertoires used to read and write within and across societies.

Canagarajah (2013) reminds us that there is a long history of individuals and societies that have used more than one language to communicate orally and in writing. He stresses that in today's globalized world, transnational contact, through migration and technological developments, has augmented exposure to and use of divergent languages, texts, and linguistic modes to think and communicate ideas.

Biliteracy is understood as a greater and more complex form of literacy than monoliteracy (Hopewell & Escamilla, 2014). Bialystok, Luk, & Kwan (2005) found that bilingualism influences literacy acquisition, making this process uniquely different from monolingual acquisition of literacy. Their research suggests that (a) "bilinguals develop several of the background skills for literacy differently from monolinguals" and (b) "bilinguals may have the opportunity to transfer the skills acquired for reading in one language to reading in the other" (p. 44).

RE-ENVISIONING INSTRUCTION FROM A BILITERACY PERSPECTIVE

García (2009) explains that biliteracy instruction usually follows one of two main approaches: sequential or simultaneous. According to Escamilla and colleagues (2014), instruction in many schools follows a sequential model. That is, students learn to read in one language before they learn to read in the other.

An additional characteristic of this model is that languages are kept separate during instruction. There is one lesson for teaching reading in Spanish and a different lesson to teach reading in English. These researchers observe that there is from none to minimal co-planning between teachers and that the use of different curriculum is stressed. Research on multilingual literacy done with sequential bilinguals, although not extensive, suggests that teaching children to read in English and Spanish promotes biliteracy, as well as higher levels of reading achievement in English (August & Shanahan, 2006; Rolstad, Mahoney, & Glass, 2005; Slavin & Cheung, 2005, as cited in Escamilla et al., 2014).

Interestingly, other researchers have found that bilingual reading approaches, where both languages are taught and used to teach reading and writing simultaneously, are also effective in helping children learn to read and write in two languages (Edelsky, 1986; Hudelson, 1987; Velasco & García, 2014). Multilingual literacy approaches to instruction stress the use of transition strategies by teachers to monitor and guide shifts across languages (August & Shanahan, 2006; Goldenberg, 2008).

To achieve multilingual literacy approaches, Escamilla and colleagues (2014) suggest discussions on the use of cognates and analyzing writing across languages. Beeman and Urow (2013) recommend designing biliteracy units that use the bridge (a time when students are taught to examine the similarities and differences between languages using contrastive analysis) as an instructional tool to develop students' cross-linguistic skills (p. 50).

Researchers have argued that instruction should maximize the bidirectional transfer of students' knowledge and skills from the first language (L1) to the second language (L2) and from the L2 to the L1 (Cummins, 1979; Dickinson, McCabe, Clark-Chiarelli, & Wolf, 2004; Fishman, 1980; Mace-Matluck, 1982; Reyes, 2001; Talebi, 2013). The fact is that language allocation in the biliteracy classroom can be multiform. García (2009) identifies four models of language and literacy use in biliteracy instruction where teachers need to make decisions about what and how languages are used in literacy.

1. A *convergent monoliterate model*, which uses the two languages in communication to transact with a text written in one language, usually a dominant one.
2. A *convergent biliterate model*, which uses the two languages in communication to transact with a text written in each of the two languages, but with literacy practices taught in the less dominant language shaped by the literacy practices used in the dominant language.
3. A *separation biliterate model*, which uses one language or the other to transact with a text written in one language or the other according to their own sociocultural and discourse norms.

4. A *flexible multiple model*, which uses the two languages in communication to transact with texts written in both languages and in other media according to a bilingual flexible norm, capable of both integration and separation (p. 342).

Finally, based on these early conceptualizations of biliteracy models, Escamilla and her colleagues (2014) recently highlighted the potential of approaches like the *"paired literacy" concurrent approach to multilingual literacy instruction* in English and Spanish. This approach draws on all the children's bilingual competencies and engages in cross-language connections.

To illustrate, a reading lesson could implement methods and instructional activities where the students guided by the teacher make comparisons across languages. The teacher may choose to read in Spanish first, demonstrating a reading strategy like using context clues for comprehension, and, at some point of the lesson, discuss the same reading strategy as it is used in English.

LINGUISTIC INTEGRATION WHEN TEACHING CONTENT

The research literature synthesized above challenges bilingual educators to consider integrative views of literacy in more than one language and to implement contemporary instructional approaches, which insightfully mix languages to navigate written texts. Given contemporary understandings of multilingual literacy, pedagogical practices used to implement multilingual academic literacy are explored.

Three bilingual elementary charter schools (third to fifth grades) located in an urban school district in a northeastern state of the United States served as the setting. The discussion that follows captures practices that are reflective of the linguistic integrative perspective on bilingual instruction in school contexts that favor language separation.

Ms. Uva and Ms. Rocio (pseudonyms are used for proper names) teach social studies and Spanish language arts in an 80-minute block at School A, an elementary bilingual, dual-language charter school. Ms. Uva teaches third grade, and Ms. Rocio works with fourth graders. Administrators at this school advocate for language separation in instruction.

Ms. Prenda, Ms. Pajal, and Mr. Granja teach in School B, an elementary bilingual, dual-language charter school. They all teach social studies and Spanish language arts in an 80-minute block. Mr. Granja teaches in third grade, Ms. Prenda in fourth grade, and Ms. Pajal in fifth grade. The language that the school administration expects the teachers to use for instruction is Spanish. Also, the school administrators require maintaining language separation in the classroom, that is, all instruction should be conducted in Spanish, no code-switching and translation to English is encouraged.

Ms. Robles is a bilingual teacher at School C, also an elementary bilingual, dual-language charter school. She teaches a fifth-grade class in a self-contained bilingual classroom, allocating language of instruction by content. Science, English language arts, and mathematics are taught in English, and social studies and Spanish language arts are taught in Spanish. Administrators at this school, as with the other two schools, believe that language separation in instruction is necessary for developing bilingualism and biliteracy.

All three schools share very similar student demographics. That is, the students come from mostly Latino homes where they have been exposed to Spanish language and attended preschool where they began to acquire English, their additional language. These types of students are identified in the literature as simultaneous bilinguals (Baker, 2011), since their acquisition process of two or more languages begins before they enter school at age five.

Mrs. Sandoval explains, "The students are second- and third-generation Latinos with a few first generation and recent immigrants" (School B, November 2014 interview). Most understand Spanish when spoken to, but have difficulty reading and writing it. For the majority, English is the dominant language socially and academically.

There are also a handful of students from Arabic- and Haitian-Creole-speaking, recent-immigrant homes. Finally, there are a few African American and Chinese students who are learning Spanish as a second or third language.

Observations of instruction in all the schools point to the use of sequential models of biliteracy instruction, where languages are kept separate during instruction. There is one class for teaching reading in Spanish, taught by one teacher, and a class to teach reading in English, instructed by a different teacher.

The choice of sequential instruction is significant since, as previously mentioned, the majority of the students in the schools are simultaneous bilinguals, that is, they are exposed to both languages between birth and age five (i.e., at home both languages are used or at home one language is used and at school the other is used) and students develop some proficiency in both oral and written language. The model used to teach literacy in two languages seems to be at odds with the home experiences the students have had learning the two languages simultaneously.

However, as documented through observations some teachers use *integrative linguistic pedagogy* to promote bilingualism and biliteracy development. The teachers at the three schools acknowledge their students' simultaneous use of both languages and a need to scaffold comprehension of content presented in Spanish. Accordingly, they include integrative linguistic practices within a sequential model of instruction that endorses language separation.

This practice suggests the notion that these teachers follow a *convergent monoliterate model* (García, 2009) for language and literacy instruction. That is, the teachers instruct in two languages to guide students in negotiating text written in Spanish. In the examples below, the teachers use Spanish and some English to support students' creation of meaning from oral discourse and written text in Spanish. Specifically, the integrative linguistic practices observed included: (1) translation; (2) small group work in a language different from the instructional one; (3) instruction of cognates; (4) no reteaching of concepts across languages; (5) metalinguistic awareness; and (6) code-switching. While individual practices were observed in the six classrooms, none of the teachers implemented all of them in their instruction.

Ms. Prenda integrates languages by *translating*. When she gives directions before an activity students need to complete, she will first give them in Spanish and ask for understanding. Then she will explain in English any part of the directions that students mentioned they could not understand. After that, she will repeat the directions in Spanish. As she explained, "I see it as necessary [for comprehension] at the moment during class. . . . I believe that translating helps these students if I use it strategically. When I know that no one knows the word or what I am saying, then it is important to translate. Many students get it immediately and others need more practice" (Ms. Prenda, School B, September 2014).

Ms. Robles translates specific academic language that is beyond students' proficiency in Spanish. When teaching, she will stop to explain a word in Spanish, give the English translation, and continue with the lesson in Spanish. Swinney and Velasco (2011) identify this strategy as *explanations on the run* (p. 11). Ms. Robles adapts this strategy by adding the English translation.

For instance, one Chinese student in her classroom was reading aloud in Spanish. She stopped reading when she did not recognize a word. Ms. Robles waited before asking the student in Spanish to divide the word into syllables.

Aloud the student said *a-sin-tió*. Then the teacher asked her to put all the syllables together and say *asintió* (agreed). After the student repeated, saying the word twice, the teacher asked the student if she knew the meaning of the word. As the student did not, the teacher provided the quick definition in Spanish and then translated it into English, before asking the student to think about the meaning and continue reading orally in Spanish.

By doing this, the teachers successfully model the bidirectional transfer between languages (Talebi, 2013) and how languages network with one another (Sebba, 2012). According to Escamilla and colleagues (2014), translation is a useful cross-language strategy. It promotes the use of languages in an interconnected way. Also, these authors cite the work of Orellana, Martínez, Lee, and Montaño (2013) to indicate that successful translations may support the acquisition of higher-order skills and the development of bilingual/biliterate proficiency. They also distinguished between literal (i.e., carro/car) and conceptual translations (i.e., idioms).

The translations observed in both classrooms were mostly at the literal level. Reyes & Kleyn (2009) acknowledge the need to translate sometimes in the bilingual classroom. Yet they do not support the use of concurrent translation because they perceive children tune out one language when everything is translated.

The examples presented show how the two teachers use translation sporadically as a comprehension scaffold. The pattern for translation followed points to instruction in Spanish, translate to English the word or phrase not understood, and then repeat in Spanish. The teachers translated when students lacked understanding of specific words as part of giving directions and when students read aloud. In both classrooms, the teachers translated from Spanish to English and from English to Spanish.

Another way that teachers integrate languages is by allowing students to *share and discuss in a language different from the language of instruction* when working in small groups. Langer, Bartolomé, Vasquez, and Lucas (1990) explain that the process of acquiring an L2 in addition to the L1 involves thinking in the L1 to make sense of the written text being read in the L2. It has been found that thinking of words and ideas in the dominant language is used as a comprehension aid when reading difficult text in the less dominant language (Cloud, Genesee, & Hamayan, 2009).

Thus, allowing students in the bilingual classes observed to process ideas in English before they express them in Spanish is a useful strategy in supporting bilingualism and biliteracy. Students' conceptual development is strengthened when they can explore concepts in L1 before having to discuss them in their L2 (Brisk & Proctor, 2012). The need to use this linguistic scaffold for comprehension will diminish as students become more proficient in the additional language.

The observations pointed to two teachers who allowed students to use some English to discuss concepts while working in small groups. All the teachers observed emphasized small group work. Particularly, Mr. Granja and Ms. Rocio constantly encouraged and reminded students to use Spanish during group work. While they allowed some use of English in the small group work, they required students to present their answers to the whole class only in Spanish.

For example, Mr. Granja was teaching a poem in Spanish that identified important values the school promoted. He instructed third-grade students to work in groups to identify real situations that could exemplify the values presented in the poem. As part of giving directions for this activity, he reminded students to discuss as much as they could in Spanish. If a student could not think of a word in Spanish, they could say it in English, but someone else in the group needed to translate to Spanish.

While students worked in small groups, he congratulated those students he heard using Spanish, yet he did not reprimand when students used English in their discussion. At times students shared an idea in English and then asked one another "*cómo se dice . . . ?*" (How do you say . . . ?). They would also discuss ideas in English and work together to write them down in Spanish. When students shared their ideas with the whole class, they spoke in Spanish. Again, when they could not think of a word in Spanish, they would ask the teacher, "cómo se dice . . ." This strategy allowed them to complete their thoughts in Spanish.

Mr. Granja explained that students' proficiency in Spanish varies across students, so he tries to create groups of mixed linguistic abilities. He also stresses the use of Spanish in the class, while allowing some English to be used in small groups' discussions. He explained that,

> It is necessary for students to complete their thoughts, what they want to say. Then, they can ask for the word in Spanish, you know, to say their thoughts orally in Spanish after they process them in English. Many of them are at a stage where they need to process thoughts in English first and then translate to Spanish. It is a process; I understand the process. However, I insist that they have to speak Spanish to the whole class. (Mr. Granja, September 2014 interview)

Ms. Rocio uses a similar procedure in her fourth-grade class. In her classroom she accepts that students ask her, "cómo se dice . . . " and use this strategy with one another when working in small groups. When an answer is given in English, she insists that students must repeat the answer using only Spanish.

To illustrate, one day her class was having a whole group discussion on cause and effect after having read and discussed a text in Spanish about Nelson Mandela in small groups. One student was explaining an incident of a group protest. He stated in English, "the people were protesting in front of a building." The teacher said, "good answer, now say it in Spanish." He remarked he did not know how to say "building" in Spanish. When he asked for help, one student said "*edificio*," while another said "*rascacielo*."

Rather than allowing the student to continue with his discussion, the teacher asked him to say the full statement again using only Spanish. The student stated, "*Las personas estaban protestando en frente del edificio*" (The people were protesting in front of the building).

By allowing students to process learning of academic content in English before expressing their learning in Spanish, these students can see how skills and strategies interact dynamically across languages. They can also put to use their rich linguistic repertoire to negotiate and transact text.

Another integrative strategy is to *teach cognates*. According to Swinney and Velasco, "Cognates are words that share the same linguistic roots; this means that they look very similar in written language" (2011, p. 17). Academic text with technical words contains many cognates between English and Spanish. These authors point to the work of Snow, Griffin, and Burns (2005), who conclude that about two-thirds of the words across these languages are cognates. They argue that teaching cognates can help students to develop the academic vocabulary of nonfiction texts across languages.

The observations showed that all the teachers called attention to cognates in their instruction. In particular, as part of reading social studies or language arts text, Mr. Granja frontloads cognate instruction (Swinney & Velasco, 2011). He does it to develop background knowledge of vocabulary and to expand students' understanding of text.

For instance, as he teaches a poem, he identifies cognates and discusses their meaning in Spanish (i.e., *comunidad*/community; *académica*/academic; *soluciones*/solutions; *creativas*/creative; *responsabilidad*/responsibility; *honestidad*/honesty; and *cooperación*/cooperation). He reads the entire poem in Spanish once, then he asks students to read aloud with him, and then, as he underlines the cognates one-by-one, he asks for the words in English and discusses their meaning. When asked about frontloading cognates, he comments that,

> It is important to take advantage of the *cognados* [cognates]; I want students to learn to recognize them, but to also know that the meaning does not change across languages. When I insist that they not only identify the similarities between words that are cognates, but that they also look and check that the meaning is the same, I am helping them to build their comprehension. Also, I am guiding them to learn about false cognates. They always react when we check the meaning of two words that look the same but their meaning is different. That is why we always need to do both, look at the linguistic similarity and at the meaning. (Mr. Granja, September 23, 2014, interview)

August and Shanahan (2006) and Goldenberg (2008) believe that it is important for students to make transitions across languages. By working on identifying cognates across both languages, similarities and differences are explained and vocabulary growth in both languages is promoted. In particular, cognates build growth in vocabulary doublets (Oller, Pearson, & Cobo-Lewis, 2007). These are words students know the meaning of and can use in both languages (Pearson, Fernández, & Oller, 1993).

An additional characteristic of good practice in multilingual literacy instruction is *not to teach the same concepts, skills, and strategies in both languages.* According to Cummins (2005), concepts can be transferred across languages.

Teachers can diagnose the background knowledge of students to recognize when students already know concepts learned in one language, and then create conditions during lessons for their transfer into the other language. Rather than teaching the same concept in two languages, teachers can use the students' previous linguistic, content, skill, strategic, and conceptual knowledge developed in one language to expand their understanding in the other language (Beeman & Urow, 2013).

This recommended practice was observed in Ms. Rocio's class (fourth grade, School A). During the lesson mentioned above about the life of Nelson Mandela, she required students to analyze the text critically, making cause and effect connections. She asked students in Spanish, "Ok, I read the last two paragraphs and now I want you to analyze them thinking what caused Mr. Mandela to laugh at the police of the jail where he was. Remember what we studied last week about cause and effect." One student, who exclaimed in Spanish, interrupted her,

> "Mandela remembered how ignorant the blacks and whites were about the apartheid system. He was not laughing at them, but at the reason for the fear of the policemen." Another student exclaimed in Spanish, "They did not trust black people because they had been taught not to trust them." The teacher responded in Spanish, "Yes, oh my goodness, you already know about cause and effect, let's move on then, what other cause and effect analysis can you make in these two paragraphs."

At the end of class I asked this teacher about the exchange, and she explained, "I was not sure if the students knew the analytical skill of cause and effect. For some it might be completely new, but for others it was taught in the English class last week, but they might not remember. As they showed me today, I do not have to reteach it; they were able to remember the skill and I can simply use it when we read in Spanish" (Ms. Rocio, October 2014 interview).

An additional strategy is one that researchers have identified as *developing metalinguistic awareness* of bilingual learners. Metalanguage is needed for children to develop an understanding of and ability to talk about language both within and across language systems (Escamilla et al., 2014). These authors explain that, "the development of metalanguage includes the ability to identify, analyze, and manipulate language forms, and to analyze sounds, symbols, grammar, vocabulary, and language structures between and across languages" (p. 67).

During a lesson on punctuation marks in Spanish to fifth graders, Ms. Pajal (School B) directed students to identify four types of statements and necessary punctuation marks. Students working independently proceeded to complete the task. After ten minutes, the teacher started to discuss the exercise and commented in Spanish: "Notice how in Spanish we use two punctuation marks to indicate an interrogative statement (as she wrote them down on the board). And in English how many do we use? Yes, only one and where do we put it; aha, only at the end of the question (she did not write the English marks, just made an oral comment). Very good."

The teacher's comment compared the use of punctuation marks between Spanish and English. When asked about this activity, she explained that at times she would compare punctuation and word meanings across languages because the curriculum that she uses in Spanish literacy encourages these types of explanations for students.

In another lesson, the teacher wrote on the board the verb *"mirar"* (to look) and next to it she wrote a definition, *"ver u ojear,"* and showed two illustrations of children looking at a sunset. One student raised his hand to ask, "Why do you use a letter 'u' between ver and ojear?" The teacher explained in Spanish that you cannot use "o" in front of a word that begins with "o" like "ojear", thus you put a "u" instead. In Spanish, we can use "o" or "u" to signify that you have an option, but in English you only use "or" like to say, "Choose either this one or that one."

The teacher explained her thinking about the comparison/contrasting activity. She said,

> It is good for them to know that in English you only use one punctuation mark and in Spanish two, because when they write they need to know this. Also, the children themselves are curious about language use that does not follow a rule, like the use of "o" and "u." I took advantage of that opportunity to contrast the languages. That helps the students become more flexible in their language use when communicating in Spanish and English. It shows them that it is OK when the word used in Spanish does not exist in English, or vice versa, or when a rule in Spanish does not exist in English or vice versa. They see that to communicate it is not just important to know the words in each language, but they have to know how language works, how each language works. (Ms. Pajal, November 2014 interview)

Beeman and Urow (2013) explain that, "By explicitly teaching, talking about, and naming elements of language within a comprehensible context, the teacher is fostering metalinguistic awareness" (p. 50). They also suggest that all the linguistic resources of students are used independently when teachers implement this cross-linguistic activity.

Code-switching across languages by students and the teachers was the final integrative strategy observed. Although all teachers encouraged and reminded students to use Spanish orally and in writing, they allowed them to respond and comment in English or to code-switch in English and in Spanish during lessons. Also, while most of the instruction in all classrooms was done in Spanish, at times some teachers would switch between English and Spanish.

It is important to note that on these instances, the purpose of the teacher was not to translate because the students did not understand, but to communicate ideas switching across languages. In this way, academic communication used the different linguistic resources of the students and the teachers.

Particularly, in Ms. Uva, Mr. Granja, and Ms. Pajal's classrooms, the students may have asked a question in English but the teacher would always answer in Spanish. In Mr. Granja's classroom, a student answered a question code-switching and the teacher validated her answer in Spanish. The student said, "Maestro tú estas contando por 'two,' by two." The teacher responded, "Si, yo estoy contando por dos" (Yes, I am counting by two). He continued with the lesson speaking in Spanish.

Ms. Rocio encourages her students to answer in Spanish and allows them to code-switch, using as much Spanish as they can. This was clearly seen in lessons where students answered questions after reading texts in Spanish about slavery and another on poems. They answered, "*un building*" (a building), "*los slaves*" (the slaves), and "*eso es como el libro que leimos about narrative poems*" (Is like the book we read about narrative poems).

Both Ms. Robles and Ms. Prajal code-switched in their instruction and they allowed students to code-switch when answering questions in class. In a lesson about César Chavez, Ms. Robles asked students to make connections to their own lives, and one student answered, "*Maestra, yo camino en un march de autism*" (Teacher, I walked in an awareness march on autism). The teacher responded in Spanish, "Yes, I am glad you made a good connection," and continued with the lesson.

Most often, Ms. Prajal would remind students to answer in Spanish; however, at times during instruction she would also code-switch. To illustrate, in a morning exercise she commented, "*Hoy Leslie turns ten, cumple diez años*" (Leslie turns ten today). Her instruction continued to be done in Spanish.

Code-switching is not an instructional strategy that is supported by the administration of the schools observed. They fear that it might reflect a deficit in language use and that it might impede the strong acquisition of languages and the development of bilingualism. However, the teachers use it as a strategy to support students' communication of ideas in academic discussions. They see it as a normal communication strategy among bilinguals.

The intent of code-switching is not to translate, but to communicate ideas without interruptions, and educators should not see it as a deficit, but as an advantageous instructional strategy. Its purpose allows students to speak their ideas about the content being discussed without sacrificing meaning and being limited by any specific language. In support of code-switching, Brown

Chapter Three 51

and Larson-Hall (2012) argue that, "part of being bilingual is that the person is able to mix languages, and can do so (or not) as he or she chooses" (p. 22).

García (2009) explains code-switching as a form of *translanguaging* that allows bilinguals to use their linguistic creativity in communicating thought. Escamilla and colleagues (2014) view it as a cross-linguistic strategy that builds on metalinguistic skills and that showcases the many linguistic resources bilinguals use to communicate.

RECOMMENDATIONS FOR ACTION

The findings of this case study suggest that the relationship between multilingualism and literacy is complex. The process of developing biliteracy needs to consider language acquisition and language use, literacy skills and strategies, the school context where instruction happens, and the teachers' previous pedagogical preparation and experiences as bilinguals.

A continued advancement in the scholarly understanding of biliteracy and its instruction has challenged previous emphasis on maintaining a complete separation of languages. Currently, opportunities to integrate strategically all the linguistic resources at the disposal of students and teachers are favored in instruction. This study uncovered six instructional strategies, which integrate Spanish and English used in lessons to promote both content learning and development of bilingualism and biliteracy. The teachers in the study created instructional spaces for the integration of languages in bilingual classrooms. This validated students' construction of meaning in academic content by using a linguistic integrative perspective in teaching language and content.

These strategies are specified below, and action steps educators may take to implement them using an integrative lens are also described.

1. Show linguistic creativity by creating opportunities for students and teachers to translate for one another and code-switch to communicate ideas. Be strategic about when and how to translate and code-switch. Their implementation should not be done as an instructional routine without a focus on building meaning and generating spaces for students to communicate understanding and thought. Model and reinforce the use of both to enhance students' comprehension of these deliberate purposes.
2. Promote cross-linguistic abilities in instruction by asking students to identify cognates with their meaning. Allow discussions during pair

and small group work to be done in either language, while guiding students to share findings with the whole class in the language of instruction. In these ways, meaning and content learning can be supported at the same time that language development is reinforced. Students will negotiate content learning in their dominant language, and they will transfer the knowledge gained to the emerging language in order to communicate it to others.

3. Use strategic instruction by refraining from teaching the same content and skills across languages and by using contrastive analysis of content text to explore similarities and differences between languages and academic discourses. Content knowledge needs to be scaffolded across languages rather than repeated. Identifying language structures, critical to comprehending text, and analyzing them across languages can support the development of academic vocabulary, morphology, syntax, discourse, and meaning across languages.

RELEVANT RESOURCES

In addition to the sources included in the References, practitioners will find the resources included in this last section useful to expand their skill in implementing an integrative linguistic pedagogy.

Resources on Linguistic Creativity and Translanguaging

García, O., Ibarra Johnson, S., & Seltzer, K. (2016). *The translanguaging classroom. Leveraging students' bilingualism for learning*. Philadelphia, PA: Caslon Publishers.

García, O., & Kleyn, T. (Eds.). (2016). *Translanguaging with multilingual students: Learning from Classroom Moments*. New York: Routledge.

Contrastive Analysis

Shatz, M., & Wilkinson, L. C. (2013). *Understanding language in diverse classrooms: A primer for all teachers*. New York: Routledge.

Strategic Instruction and Cross-Linguistic Abilities

Beeman, K., & Urow, C. (2013). *Teaching for biliteracy: Strengthening bridges between languages*. Philadelphia, PA: Caslon Publishing.

Escamilla, K., Hopewell, S., Butvilofsky, S., Sparrow, W., Soltero-González, L., Ruiz-Figueroa, O., & Escamilla, M. (2014). *Biliteracy from the start: Literacy squared in action*. Philadelphia, PA: Caslon Publishing.

Website with Videos

The CUNY-NYSIEB Initiative on Emergent Bilinguals website http://www.cuny-nysieb.org/ .

REFERENCES

August, D., & Shanahan, T. (Eds.). (2006). *Developing literacy in second-language learners: Report of the National Literacy Panel on language-minority children and youth*. Mahwah, NJ: Lawrence Erlbaum.

Baker, C. (2011). *Foundations of bilingual education and bilingualism* (5th ed.). Clevedon, UK: Multilingual Matters.

Beeman, K., & Urow, C. (2013). *Teaching for biliteracy: Strengthening bridges between languages*. Philadelphia, PA: Caslon Publishing.

Bialystok, E., Luk, G., & Kwan, E. (2005). Bilingualism, biliteracy, and learning to read: Interactions among languages and writing systems. *Scientific Studies of Reading, 9* (1), 43–61.

Brisk, M. E., & Proctor, C. P. (2012). *Challenges and supports for English language learners in bilingual programs*. Paper Presented at the Understanding Language Conference. Palo Alto: Stanford University.

Brown, S., & Larson-Hall, J. (2012). *Second language acquisition myths: Applying second language research to classroom teaching*. Ann Arbor, Michigan: University of Michigan Press.

Canagarajah, A. S. (Ed.). (2013). *Literacy as translingual practice: Between communities and classrooms*. New York: Routledge.

Cenoz, J., & Gorter, D. (2011). Focus on multilingualism: A study of trilingual writing. *The Modern Language Journal, 95*(3), 356–369.

Cloud, N., Genesee, F., & Hamayan, E. (2009). *Literacy instruction for English language learners*. Portsmouth, NJ: Heinemann.

Cummins, J. (1979). Linguistic interdependence and the educational development of bilingual children. *Review of Educational Research, 49*, 222–251.

Cummins, J. (2005). Teaching for cross-language transfer in dual language education: Possibilities and pitfalls. *TESOL Symposium on Dual Language Education: Teaching and Learning Two Languages in the EFL Setting*. September 23, 2005, Boğaziçi University, Istanbul, Turkey.

de Jong, E. J. (2011). *Foundations for multilingualism in education: From principles to practice*. Philadelphia, PA: Caslon Publishing.

Dickinson, D. K., McCabe, A., Clark-Chiarelli, N., & Wolf, A. (2004). Cross-language transfer of phonological awareness in low-income Spanish and English bilingual preschool children. *Applied Psycholinguistics, 25*(3), 323–347. doi:10.1017/S0142716404001158.

Edelsky, C. K. (1986). *Writing in a bilingual program. Había una vez*. Norwood, NJ: Ablex Publishing.

Escamilla, K., Hopewell, S., Butvilofsky, S., Sparrow, W., Soltero-González, L., Ruiz-Figueroa, O., & Escamilla, M. (2014). *Biliteracy from the start: Literacy squared in action*. Philadelphia, PA: Caslon Publishing.

Fishman, J. (1980). Ethnocultural dimensions in the acquisition and retention of biliteracy. *Journal of Basic Writing, 3*, 48–61.

García, O. (2009). *Bilingual education in the 21st century: A global perspective*. Malden, MA: Wiley-Blackwell.

Goldenberg, C. (2008). Teaching English language learners: What the research does—and does not—say. *American Educator*, 8–44.
Grosjean, F. (2008). *Studying bilinguals*. New York: Oxford University Press.
Hopewell, S., & Escamilla, K. (2014). Biliteracy development in immersion contexts. *Journal of Immersion and Content-based Language Education, 2*(2), 181–195.
Hudelson, S. (1987). The role of native language literacy in the education of language minority children. *Language Arts, 64*(8), 827–841.
Langer, J. A., Bartolomé, L., Vasquez, O., & Lucas, T. (1990). Meaning construction in school literacy tasks: A study of bilingual students. *American Educational Research Journal, 27*, 427–471.
Mace-Matluck, B. J. (1982, June). Literacy instruction in bilingual settings: A synthesis of current research. (Professional Papers M-1. Los Alamitos, CA: National Center for Bilingual Research). (ERIC Document Reproduction Service No. ED 222 079).
Mancilla-Martínez, J., Pan, B. A., & Vagh, S. V. (2011). Assessing the productive vocabulary of Spanish-English bilingual toddlers from low-income families. *Applied Psycholinguistics, 32*, 333–357. doi:10.1017/S0142716410000433.
Moll, L. C., Sáez, R., & Dworin, J. (2001). Exploring biliteracy: Two student case examples of writing as a social practice. *The Elementary School Journal, 101*(4), 435–449.
New London Group (1996). A pedagogy of multiliteracies: Designing social futures. *Harvard Educational Review, 66*(*1*), 60–92.
Oller, D. K. (2005). ISB4: Proceedings of the 4th International Symposium on Bilingualism, ed. James Cohen, Kara T. McAlister, Kellie Rolstad, and Jeff MacSwan, 1744–1749. Somerville, MA: Cascadilla.
Oller, D. K., Pearson, B. C., & Cobo-Lewis, A. B. (2007). Profile effects in early bilingual language and literacy. *Applied Psycholinguist, 28*(2), 191–230. doi:10.1017/S0142716407070117.
Orellana, M. F., Martinez, D. C., Lee, C. H., & Montaño, E. (2013). "Language as a tool in diverse forms of learning": Corrigendum. *Linguistics and Education, 24*, 272. doi:10.1016/j.linged.2013.01.002.
Pearson, B. Z., Fernández, S., & Oller, D. K. (1993). Lexical development in bilingual infants and toddlers: Comparison to monolingual norms. *Language Learning, 43*, 93–120.
Pearson, B. Z., Fernández, S., & Oller, D. K. (1995). Cross language synonyms in the lexicons of bilingual infants: One language or two? *Journal of Child Language, 22*, 345–368.
Pearson, B. Z., & Fernández, S. C. (1994). Patterns of interaction in the lexical development in two languages of bilingual infants. *Language Learning, 44*(4), 617–653.
Poulin-Dubois, D., Bialystok, E., Blaye, A., Polonia, A., & Yott, J. (2012). Lexical access and vocabulary development in very young bilinguals. *International Journal of Bilingualism*. doi: 1367006911431198.
Reyes, M. (2001). Unleashing possibilities: Biliteracy in the primary grades. In M. Reyes & J. Halcón (Eds.), *The best for our children: Critical perspectives on literacy for Latino students*. New York: Teachers College Press.
Reyes, S. A., & Kleyn, T. (2009). *Teaching in two languages: A guide for K–12 bilingual educators*. Thousand Oaks, CA: Corwin Press.
Rolstad, K., Mahoney, K., & Glass, G. V. (2005). The big picture: A meta analysis of program effectiveness research on English language learners. *Educational Policy, 19*, 572–594.
Sebba, M. (2012). Multilingualism in written discourse: An approach to the analysis of multilingual texts. *International Journal of Bilingualism, 17*, 97–118. doi:10.1177/1367006912438301.

Slavin, R. E., & Cheung, A. (2005). A synthesis of research on language of reading instruction for English language learners. *Review of Educational Research, 75*(2), 247–284.

Snow, C. E., Griffin, P., Burns, M. S., and the NAE Subcommittee on Teaching Reading. (2005). *Knowledge to support the teaching of reading: Preparing teachers for a changing world.* San Francisco, CA: Jossey Bass.

Swinney, R., & Velasco, P. (2011). *Connecting content and academic language for English learners and struggling students, grades 2–6.* Thousand Oaks, CA: Corwin Press.

Talebi, S. H. (2013). Cross-linguistic transfer (from L1 to L2, L2 to L1, and L2 to L3) of reading strategies in a multicompetent mind. *Journal of Language Teaching and Research, 4*(2), 432–436. doi:10.4304/jltr.4.2.432-436.

Velasco, P., & García, O. (2014). Translanguaging and the writing of bilingual learners. *Bilingual Research Journal, 37*(1), 6–23.

Part Two

Considerations for Examining and Supporting Language Development

Chapter Four

Language Is a Resource: Revaluing Readers' Transliteracies through Miscue Analysis and Retrospective Miscue Analysis (RMA)

Yetta Goodman and Kelly Allen

Exploring language learning and Richard Ruiz's language orientation, language as a resource, is central to establishing the rights of all language learners to participate in a life of joyful discoveries and learning. Authors present a language as resource-pedagogy of miscue and retrospective miscue analysis that recognizes and respects readers' linguistic strengths and diverse and rich literacy experiences as language and literacy resources that revalue, expand, and promote literacy. Literacy and language instruction and curriculum designed to promote second-language learning benefits learners when students' language is honored, where literacy is seen as social and cultural, where literacy is developed and supported as a language process, and where teachers and learners come together as partners and collaborators in language learning.

After a parents' literacy support group at a university where young readers attended a daily literacy workshop, the mother of a third-grade student stayed behind after the other parents had left. She said worriedly, almost pleadingly, "I know I need to read to Marisela everyday but I don't want to stop reading to her in Spanish. I know that reading in English would help both of us with our pronunciation but I really don't want to stop reading to her in Spanish."

Though this mother wanted to read in Spanish, she also inferred that for instructional purposes, she should concede reading in her own first language. Kelly assured her that she should *never* stop reading in Spanish, but reading in English would be good too. The mother could read aloud in Spanish, and her daughter could read aloud in English. In this way, Kelly, as teacher, acknowledges that literacy in Spanish is an important part of the shared life and culture of mother and daughter and makes clear the importance she places on their biliteracy.

Being *literate* isn't about mastering the dominant language, rather it is using the process of constructing meaning through written texts for appropriate purposes with appropriate language for the specific context. Bilingualism and biliteracy (Goodman, Goodman, & Flores, 1979) must be supported and respected as language strengths of the learner, and never considered evidence of language deficiency.

As this mother continues to read to her child in Spanish, she develops and affirms literacy in her cultural context and as an important part of the intellectual life of her daughter. She is expanding on her family's language strengths and resources.

Providing literacy support through thoughtful literacy instruction is built on understanding literacy as a *universal* language process (Goodman, Fries, & Strauss, 2016; Goodman, Wang, Iventosch, & Goodman, 2011). In 1984, Richard Ruiz highlighted language orientations, their importance in language learning, and the ways in which language orientations or ideologies:

> delimit the ways we talk about language and language issues, they determine the basic questions we ask, the conclusions we draw from the data, and even the data themselves. Orientations are related to *language attitudes* in that they constitute the framework in which attitudes are formed: they help to delimit the range of acceptable attitudes toward language, and to make certain attitudes legitimate. (p. 16)

Ruiz discusses language as a problem, language as a right, and, especially for the purposes of this article, *language as a resource*,—a language orientation that mitigates problems that arise from the first two orientations. According to Ruiz, as teachers enact a *language as a resource orientation* it has:

> a direct impact on enhancing the language status of subordinate languages; it can help to ease tensions between majority and minority communities; it can serve as a more consistent way of viewing the role of non-English languages in

U.S. society; and it highlights the importance of cooperative language planning. (pp. 25–26)

As we discuss literacy learning for ESL and biliterate learners, we keep the *language as a resource* concept at the center.

In ESL classrooms and programs involving second language learners and biliterates, we plan to demonstrate through engaging curriculum how students' linguistic and cultural resources and repertoires are not only valued, but necessary for learning to occur. Teachers need to involve students in consciously knowing how their first language(s) is a resource not only for the developing readers and writers but for the teacher as well.

Research acknowledges the importance of the linguistic and cultural resources bilingual and bidialectal students bring with them to school and calls for teachers to expand on these resources in curriculum and instruction (Gregory, 2008). When teachers honor students' translanguage capabilities (Creese & Blackledge, 2010; González, 2015), literacy development expands and teachers grow in their understanding of how to build upon students' capabilities.

Ruiz (1984) challenges the lack of concern over *resource conservation* and suggests "there seems to be no acknowledgement of the fact that existing resources are being destroyed through mismanagement and repression. This is true even where language communities are recognized as important reservoirs of language skills (p. 26).

By developing authentic experiences with students, teachers demonstrate the value of their students' language(s), and students come to value their own language and learning too. Students discover their own questions and problem-solving strategies as teachers engage readers with authentic materials that are of significant interest to them.

As we consider rich curricular experiences for students, we take into consideration the concept of *translanguaging* and *transliteracy* (Creese & Blackledge, 2010; González, 2015). These constructs are used in literacy research and theory to highlight the diverse and complex language environments in which humans live, work, and grow.

Conceptualizations of translanguages and transliteracy include the complexities of all language forms "across a range of platforms, tools and media from signing and orality through handwriting, print T.V., radio and film to digital social networks" (Thomas et al., 2007). Humans continuously develop language proficiencies whenever they use language in this diverse and complex language world.

Learning within a translanguaging framework focuses students on their linguistic resources—the *transliteracy* opportunities in which they engage regularly; their own knowledge, interests, questions, and concerns; and their literacy learning processes, the "communicative flow" (González, 2015)—and is not solely focused on L1 or L2 (García & Wei, 2014). Rather, it considers all language use in a range of social communities in which children and adolescents interact, take action, and learn.

Translanguaging includes the specific process of constructing meaning, the brain activity used to make sense (Goodman, Goodman, & Allen, 2016), and draws from individual's linguistic and cultural repertoires to build and construct meaning. This differs from traditional notions of learning to read and write that privilege one literacy over another such as schooled literacy versus out of school literacy, digital forms of literacy versus traditional forms of reading and writing, and dominant languages spoken in schools versus students' first languages.

"A translanguaging lens really questions the idea that there is a monolingual way" (Orellana & García, 2014, p. 388). Monolinguals are actively engaged in translanguaging with rich language variations such as oral and written language within the complexity of multiple semiotic systems (i.e., art, music) and adapt to different genre needs such as charts, lists, diagrams, drama, storytelling, jokes, and digital devices based on their learning needs.

In this chapter, we emphasize a resource pedagogy (Ruiz, 1984) to establish the power of language learning in a complex transliterate environment. We challenge deficit-based social perceptions of language, discourse, and instruction that: (1) prioritize word accuracy and fluency over comprehension; (2) delay rich literacy opportunities by requiring mastery of skills prior to real reading and writing; (3) devalue and ignore a readers' first language resources; and (4) view L1 oral and written language abilities inconsequential in learning English.

Our position is that a student's first language is a rich resource that informs and shapes the literacy process in a second language. When learners believe they are capable in their first language (L1), they are more confident to acknowledge their competence as they continue to develop English as a second language (L2 or more).

Teachers who acknowledge readers' first languages as valuable encourage students to draw from their language resources and background knowledge to support L2 English learning. Teachers continuously engage and focus readers on comprehension in *all* languages. The following principles are integral in a classroom or tutoring environment in which ESL learning takes place easily and with minimal anxiety on the part of the learner.

LANGUAGE LEARNING PRINCIPLES

1. *All humans learn language, including written language, when they need language for their own purposes. Learners are in control of their learning.*
2. *Every language that learners use and develop becomes a resource, a powerful tool to explore the world (Ruiz, 1984). However, such a powerful tool in specific contexts can have negative influences on the learner.*
3. *Reading is what the human mind does when transacting with a written text (not necessarily what is taught in traditional instruction).*
4. *Teachers' conversations with readers about their reading provide opportunities to help students revalue themselves as learners. As teachers and learners talk about a reading experience together, they become partners in teaching, learning, and revaluing.*
5. *Language, including reading, is learned in the context of its use with authentic materials for personal and social purposes.*

Principle 1: All Humans Learn Language, Including Written Language, when they Need Language for Their Own Purposes. Learners Are in Control of Their Learning.

Learning takes place continuously and occurs within specific contexts through events and experiences. Learners make decisions about which parts of their learning to assimilate and accommodate into their developing knowledge base (Goodman, 1990). When language and culture in this context are valued, learners comfortably use their knowledge and languages to become actively engaged learners. Learning strategies are already developed orally in learners' first languages (L1) long before schooling begins.

Depending on home and community language use, students develop language resources in second or third languages. Young children develop proficiency in predicting, confirming, self-correcting, making inferences, and constructing meaning as a result of connecting with family and caregivers.

They use their first language to accomplish what they want to know and say, and soon begin to read and write. When their language capabilities are acknowledged by teachers or parents, their strategies are extended to their second language(s), building and expanding their bilingual and biliterate resources.

Before schooling, young readers and writers already differentiate between written and oral language and how symbol systems such as art, music, and dance represent meanings in different ways. They know that people use different language forms in different contexts, with different people, and for different purposes.

Teachers build on what learners already know and help them realize the power of their resources. Language learners need to know they are continuously learning as they engage as speakers, readers, writers, and listeners of different languages.

Michael Halliday (2003), a systemic linguist, believes that language learning results from using language in authentic contexts with authentic materials and for real purposes of interest to the learner. He says that *whenever humans use language*—asking questions, discussing, brainstorming, listening to stories, reading from digital devices, reading print sources in the environment or in academic texts—the result is that *they learn language*; *they learn through language*: and *they learn about language*. Language is learned in the context of its use.

The individual brain is always learning. Teachers do not impose learning by telling students what and how they need to learn. Experienced teachers provide an environment rich in opportunities in which students actively engage in using language to learn language. Second-language learners use their L1 resources, their developing L2 resources, and the complexity of all the features of their transliterate world to continuously develop their literacy learning.

For example, young children show through different intonation patterns that they have learned which sentences are questions and which are statements well before they are able to articulate which sentences are *interrogative or declarative*. They focus their thinking and learning on making sense. Jamal's work shows this complexity.

Jamal wrote and drew the story below based on his teacher's suggestions to the class. Jamal spoke Arabic as his first language and was placed, at his father's request, in a bilingual Spanish/English first grade when he came to the United States. His teacher read a story about an alligator who was smoking. The teacher then invited the children to write and draw what they liked best about the story.

Jamal wrote his name in English at the top left of the page and in Arabic on the right. He drew an alligator smoking in front of a podium and the teacher smoking and reading a book behind the podium. He wrote the bottom sentence in English first, then wrote the top sentence in Spanish, and the middle sentence he wrote in Arabic.

After telling his teacher about his drawing, Jamal read the bottom line to his teacher in English: "I liked when the [*da* his phoneme for the *th* in English] lizard smoked." He read the top line in Spanish: "A mi me gustó cuando fumo" (in translation similar to English). He read the middle line to the teacher orally in Arabic (the letter forms are Arabic). The teacher was not able to translate Jamal's Arabic.

Without direct instruction, Jamal's writing illustrates language knowledge about the three languages he is learning simultaneously. In English spelling, he uses mostly consonants, and in Spanish, vowels. His grammar is appropriate. These are consistent with research findings of young writers in the invention of spellings in Spanish and English (Edelsky, 1991; Ferreiro & Teberosky, 1982). Jamal's writing demonstrates his developmental control of orthographic, grammatical, and semantic aspects of the alphabetic writing systems in English and Spanish.

Principle 2: Every Language That Learners Use and Develop Becomes a Resource, a Powerful Tool to Explore the World (Ruiz, 1984). However, Such a Powerful Tool in Specific Contexts Can Have Negative Influences on the Learner.

Students' own language learning becomes visible as teachers respect and facilitate the ways in which students speak and use their cumulative language knowledge about their world as they continually expand, build upon, and co-construct conceptual and linguistic knowledge in both L1 and L2 language(s).

However, when language learning is taken out of the context of a "meaningful whole" and placed in restricted and highly controlled contexts, with little insight into how language is learned and used, learners (readers, writers, speakers, listeners, and signers) often develop attitudes about themselves as language users that have negative impacts on their language learning throughout their lives.

Line of print in Spanish

A/ m / e /   u s o/   g a o /   Fmo

A/ mi/ me /   gusto cuando fumo

Line of print in Arabic

I/ L t/ w   /d/l z r   Smot

I/liked/when/da/lizard smoked

Jamal's house.

If learners do not recognize the importance of what they are learning, their brains are selective and choose not to learn; not to engage. Readers, regardless of age, frequently show through their miscues that instruction can focus learners' attention toward sounding out and syllabifying and away from a meaning-focused view of reading.

Joel Dworin (2003) on the other hand, researches how bilingual learners use their languages as resources to construct meaning, the ultimate goal of literacy. He describes the transliteracy nature of biliteracy development:

as a bidirectional process rather than one that only involves transfer from the first language to the second. In other words, biliteracy development is a dynamic, flexible process in which children's transactions with two written languages mediate their language learning for both languages. (p. 179–180)

The background knowledge and experiences that show language strengths and resources ESL/bilingual students use in their homes and communities often go unnoticed and rarely receive intellectual credit in traditional schooling. At home, these learners are often *language brokers* (Morales & Hanson, 2005), helping members of their families and communities understand the unfamiliar in their surroundings. They use their L1 resources to translate unique aspects of their environments and the unfamiliar to family members.

Yet when insightful teachers invite students to bring these strengths into their classrooms or to individual and small group reading conferences, to share their insights with others through a curriculum that involves inquiry, questioning, and meaning-making, teachers are able to use students' resources as well. This is why our recommendations for learning experiences in this chapter highlight teachers who involve students in rich experiences that inspire, invite, and extend learning. We use *teacher* to represent all professionals and volunteers who work with ESL and biliterate learners.

As teachers find ways to support students' strengths and show students how new learnings are appreciated and useful, second language learners become eager to share what they know and further build confidence as learners.

Here's one example: A first-grade teacher is sitting in front of an easel with a small group of bilingual children already comfortably reading in English. There is a big book on the easel with a picture of a butterfly on the cover. Across the butterfly is written MARIPOSA, and Sara calls out, "Butterfly." Other children agree, but Greg says, "No, there's no '*B*.'" Danny says, "Look, the '*M*,'" and Greg reads, "My Butterfly." Tiffany says, "My is *M Y*." Marina adds, "It starts like me, Marina." Angela reads aloud slowly, "Ma ri . . . Ma ri posa!!" Danny calls out, "It's Spanish."

During this instruction, the teacher listens intently, observes, and takes notes as children explore the cover of a new book and share their experiences with butterflies. At one point, Angela responds to Luis, "Yes, when Marina said: It starts like me. I started to say it, too, and it sounded like Spanish and I looked at the letters and it was Mariposa."

With support and open-ended discussion from the experienced teacher and the children's excited responses, the children learn about experiences and knowledge other children have with butterflies—that butterfly can't start with M; that the sound *B* is related to butterfly and made with the lips; and that mariposa sounds and looks like Spanish. As the teacher senses the discussion coming at an end, she says, "I'll open the book and start reading and we'll see how your predictions hold up." She invites the children to further explorations and assures them they will continue exploring their own understandings (Whitmore, Martens, Goodman, & Owocki, 2004).

Principle 3: Reading Is What the Human Mind Does Transacting with a Written Text (Not Necessarily What Is Taught in Traditional Instruction).

Language learners bring strategies from their earliest uses of oral language to their reading as they transact with ranges of written language genres and devices in their homes, schools, and communities. They already know what people say in specific settings and know ways to respond. They are continuously monitoring their understanding, and when they wonder how it could make sense, they ask questions and engage in self-correcting their miscues and rethinking.

The human brain uses sampling, predicting, confirming, and disconfirming strategies as the first graders demonstrated above (Goodman, Goodman, & Allen, 2016). They are asking questions to make sense, continuously expanding their learning. Readers of all languages, ages, and proficiencies miscue during reading because they are predicting and interpreting what they believe the author has written, even before they specifically see the written text. They continuously monitor their own comprehending using confirming and self-correcting strategies as they read.

Miscue analysis documents how ESL readers use the same strategies in their L1 and L2 (Crowell, 1995). Every teacher can discover the reading process by exploring their own miscues and the miscues of their students.

By conducting miscue analysis, the teacher gathers evidence of readers' miscues and reading strategies and comes to understand the role of strategies during reading. By analyzing miscues and discussing them with readers, the teacher helps readers know which miscues are of high quality and shows them how they focus on making sense, and which miscues disrupt comprehension and what strategies are most useful to focus on comprehension. In our view, reading is *making sense* or *constructing meaning*, which is synonymous with reading comprehension.

To conduct miscue analysis, readers read a complete story or article of interest. The reading is recorded, so the teacher and student are able to relisten to the reading, analyze the miscues, and discuss why the reader miscued and how miscues reveal readers' proficiency. As the reader reads, the teacher directs the reader to proceed as if reading alone.

If readers look to the teacher for support, the teacher encourages the reader to continue and do the best they can. The teacher marks miscues on a transcript of the reading. In this way, the teacher documents the kinds of strategies a reader uses and provides opportunities for readers to engage in discussions about the kinds of strategies they use when reading independently.

After reading, the teacher asks for a retelling, discusses the reading following the reader's lead, and, at a subsequent conference, shares and discusses the miscues with the reader (RMA). The recorded miscue session, including the retelling, provides opportunities to listen to selected miscues to understand what knowledge about language and the world the reader was drawing from during reading and to verify that miscues are produced by all readers regardless of proficiency.

Following the reading and retelling, the teacher listens to the recording, confirms the miscue markings (observed responses) on the story transcript, and transcribes the retelling to use in discussion about the reader's comprehension, miscues, and strategy use.

Miscue analysis research provides evidence that all readers miscue and that miscues reflect readers' knowledge and interpretation of readings. It reveals how instructional practices have influenced readers' strategies. Miscues show how the brain uses readers' predictions, confirmations, and beliefs about reading to continue comprehending throughout a text.

The following miscue excerpt is from Erica (Goodman & Anders, 1999), a bilingual Spanish/English fifth-grader reading *The Man Who Kept House* (McInnes, 1962). Erica was identified as a struggling ESL reader. The numbers to the left of each line represent the selected pages (first number in the sequence) and line numbers (second and third number) of the story where *the/her husband* and *the/his wife* occur.

We examine the miscues on *husband* in relation to *wife* to consider Erica's English-language knowledge and her reading capabilities. Erica makes no miscues on *wife*. The other miscues in these sentences are not marked since they don't relate to our focus on *husband* and *wife*.

Erica read *wife* as expected but miscues consistently on *husband* the first six times it appears (lines 108, 118, 202, 320, 601, 605), demonstrating the initial strategy she tries (sounding out when she comes to something unfamil-

106	"I keep house," replied the wife...
	uc *hub-b* ^{2}
	h- ^{1}
108	"Hard work!" said the husband.
117	... look after the baby," said the wife.
	uc *- bad* ^{2}
	hubble-bad ^{1}
118	"I can do all that," replied the husband.
201	So the next morning the wife went...
	hubbleba- ^{2}
	hubbleman ^{1}
202	The husband stayed home and
203	began to do his wife's work.
	hus-bed ^{2}
	hus- ^{1}
320	Just as the husband was putting the
601	baby crying, and her (husband) shouting for
602	help.
604	the cow fell down to the ground, and the
	huns-bad ^{1}
605	husband dropped head first down the chimney.
606	When the wife went into the house, she
	R
607	saw her husband with his legs up the
608	chimney and his head in the porridge pot.
609	From that day on, the husband went into
610	the forest every day to cut wood. The wife
611	stayed home to keep house and look
612	after their child.

(R=repeated, UC=uncorrected (word surrounded by parens omitted) (numbering next to miscue indicates 1st or second response)

Figure 4.2. *The Man Who Kept House.*

iar). However, when she divided husband into two syllables appropriately, she used features of the husband's personality in the second syllable as a compound (notice *bad*, *man*, and *bed)*. On line 601, Erica omits husband, and then in line 607, she looks up at the teacher to show she knows she finally read *her husband* out loud. The last time (line 609) *the husband* occurs, she reads it without hesitation and with appropriate sentence intonation.

We believe her miscues on *husband* relate to the unusual use of determiners (the, his, her). The author does not use names for characters in the story, preferring impersonal uses of *the husband* and *the wife*. The use of *her* prior to husband on lines 601 and 607 and *his* prior to wife on line 203 are grammatical cues in the written language that provide Erica with sufficient information to eventually read *husband*.

Careful examination of miscues within the context of an authentic reading provides information about Erica's English-language knowledge. Miscue analysis shows how readers like Erica negotiate unfamiliar linguistic units by sounding out, but when encouraged to "keep on going" and when uninterrupted during reading, Erica continues comprehending and builds enough information to produce the expected response. Erica was excited when she read husband through her own problem solving.

For the purpose of miscue analysis, every reading is followed by a retelling. Erica retold in great detail identifying with the wife and being critical of the husband. When the teacher asked Erica to expand on what the husband thought about hard work, she said:

E: He doesn't want to do hard work . . . house cleaning. The mother does hard work.

R: What do you think about hard work? Do you think that's hard?

E: No because I'm used to it.

R: Which one of them does the hard work?

E: The mother . . . And the dad because the dad works for money to keep the house and feed the children. . . . The dad does cutting wood and the lady just takes care of the house . . . and takes care of the kids.

Readers draw from textual cues as Erica does to construct meaning (Meek, 1988). Such insights help knowledgeable teachers support readers to focus on meaning-making and not on just "getting the word right." They encourage readers to monitor their reading by asking: *Does what I'm reading make sense, and if it doesn't, what can I do to make it make sense? What cues in my reading help me understand?*

Erica took ownership of her own reading and her reading strategies as she read without outside help, progressing within this one reading from less efficient to more efficient and effective reading strategies. Her complete and appropriate retelling, always part of miscue analysis, demonstrates her comprehending throughout the reading. (For a detailed profile of Erica's reading from researchers with differing perspectives, see Goodman and Anders, 1999).

Miscues provide teachers with insights into the influence of an ESL reader's first- and second-language knowledge. Although Erica did not read *husband* immediately, her awareness that she knew *husband* became evident toward the end of the story. She first relied on sounding out strategies for husband, reflecting instructional influences and her knowledge of initial, medial, and final letter/sound relations. She does not use *wife* or *husband* in her retelling, but she makes clear she understands they are *man* and *woman*; *dad* and *mother*. And the teacher has specific information to support further development of the wife/husband concept.

The teacher will encourage Erica to use her meaning-making strategies and to diminish her focus on simplistic sounding out strategies, although sounding out demonstrates her knowledge of phonics. Erica's teacher will support her strengths to keep on reading and thinking about what is happening in the story and the relationships among the characters. Using miscue analysis and retrospective miscue analysis (principle 4) provide instructional opportunities to support readers constructing meaning.

Written materials used for miscue analysis and most other reading experiences need to be authentic, whole, and long enough to explore concepts, ideas, and plot with understanding. Dorothy Menosky's research (1971) concluded that readers make more miscues that are NOT semantically and syntactically acceptable at the beginning of a reading as compared to the end of a text.

Readers use language cues throughout the text as they continue comprehending, and their miscues in the later part of their reading are of higher quality. They fit the sentence grammatically and make greater sense within the written material.

High quality miscues reveal how reading itself supports reading development. We learn to read by reading. This suggests the importance of reading material that is well written, interesting to the reader, and long enough to explore story plots or concepts. Meek's (1988) concept explores how texts teach what readers learn.

Ken Goodman's construct of miscue (1976), when a reader reads something that differs from the text, challenges word-focused models of reading. Extensive miscue research illustrates reading as the process of comprehending and documents how readers use reading strategies (Goodman & Goodman, 2014). Miscues reveal how readers are in control of their reading and how they make use of their resources: background knowledge, language cueing systems, and psycholinguistic reading strategies to construct meaning (Goodman, Goodman, & Allen, 2016).

Miscues represent interpretations that readers make continuously. Reading research describes reading as a perceptive act (K. Goodman et al., 2016). Readers make predictions dependent upon their perceptions, strategies, and focus during reading. K. Goodman and colleagues describe how "the illusion of accurate perceptions is having made sense" (p. 6).

As we see from Erica's miscues, ESL readers help teachers discover the degree to which their students are developing control over English. For example, in reading dialogue, readers expand on contractions. Fourth grader Juan made one miscue in the following sentence reading: "*Her father added, 'You do not want to be late on your first day, do you?'*" for "*You don't want to be late on your first day, do you?*" Such miscues show that the reader knows the difference between written and oral language in English.

Written language is supposed to be more formal, and the readers predict that there won't be contractions in well-written English. Sometimes, in follow-up discussions readers report not being allowed to use contractions in writing (Freeman, 2001). In instruction, following such a discussion, we involve readers to consider when and how authors use contractions in writing by keeping a notebook or file of instances during their reading when they discover contractions. Their collections are examined a few times during a semester to understand how contractions are used in real writing settings. In such explorations, students research their own language practices.

An important aspect of miscues is that teachers discover the reader's knowledge of English grammar and other language features useful for ESL teachers. For example, readers' miscues on prepositions, determiners, and conjunctions are good examples to view ESL readers' developing English grammar.

An example from an ESL third grader reading *The Man Who Kept House* substituting *him* for *her husband* explores this:

ESL Reader: When the wife went into the house she saw *her husband*

Text: When the wife went into the house she saw *him* . . . saw her husband

Proficient readers often produce such high-quality miscues and do not self-correct because the miscue makes complete sense and is acceptable in the sentence. Less confident and/or younger readers often show that they are aware of their miscue by slowing down and self-correcting before continuing to read, which this reader did.

In our discussions with readers, we focus them on making sense, comprehending, and continuing to read rather than reading slowly and carefully, reflecting their concern with accuracy. When teachers believe reading is the accurate reproduction of text, they see accuracy as a major goal and ask readers to pay close attention to the printed text. Such views are not helpful, even for proficient L1 readers.

We encourage teachers to explore their own reading through miscue analysis to continue to build understandings about the reading process. Miscue analysis provides teachers with the most important insights into the kinds of support individual readers need to continue to focus on comprehension as reading develops and, at the same time, provides a window into how the reading process works for all readers. We recommend that teachers share what they learn about reading and miscues with their students.

More complete and alternative procedures are available for conducting, documenting, and analyzing a reader's miscues (RMI) both formally and informally (Davenport, 2002; Goodman, Martens, & Flurkey, 2014; Goodman, Watson, & Burke, 2005; http://www.retrospectivemiscue.com).

Principle 4: Teachers' Conversations with Readers about Their Reading Provide Opportunities to Help Students Revalue Themselves as Learners. As Teachers and Learners Talk about a Reading Experience Together They Become Partners in Teaching, Learning, and Revaluing.

Retrospective miscue analysis (RMA) is an instructional strategy that provides readers and teachers with opportunities for thoughtful conversations about what readers do as they read and which strategies are most supportive for comprehension. The teacher initially selects 4–5 miscues from the marked miscue transcript to talk about. Both teacher and reader (individually or in a group) listen to the recorded reading for the selected miscue, following along in the transcript, and a conversation ensues in which the reader explains what she did as she was reading and why she thinks she miscued.

The teacher supports the reader asking open-ended questions: *Did the sentence you read with the miscue make sense? Why do you think so? Did you correct it? Should you have? Why do you think so?* The teacher and the reader explore together how miscues reveal the reader's strengths in making sense and comprehending (Goodman, 1996b). In sentences where meaning is disrupted, the teacher and the reader consider alternative strategies that would help the reader extend her understanding by focusing on meaning construction.

There are many ways to incorporate RMA into instruction and curriculum, formally and informally, to help readers become metacognitive and metalinguistic during reading (Crowell, 2015; Goodman, Martens, & Flurkey, 2014; 2016; Watson, 2011).

As teachers began to use miscue analysis and realized how much they were learning to support their students' reading strengths, strategies, and comprehension, they began to share what they were learning with their students. We called these experiences Retrospective Miscue Analysis (RMA) (Goodman, Martens, & Flurkey, 2016).

Teachers want readers to know that their brains are engaged in predicting and confirming almost continuously and that miscues reveal knowledge about their languages and their ability to construct meaning. Readers revalue reading (Allen & Goodman, in press) and develop confidence as their knowledge about reading and linguistic awareness grows, and at the same time, they shed deficit views of themselves as readers.

A research study using RMA as an instructional strategy with bilingual and ESL middle-school students (Goodman & Flurkey, 1996) with fourth- to eighth-grade stanine scores revealed that most of the readers initially believed that good readers read carefully, accurately, and knew every word, using sounding out and syllabication skills.

By the end of a nine-month research period of weekly RMA conferences, readers gained confidence in reading English and were able to verbalize their effective and ineffective strategies, and their test scores also improved. They revalued themselves as literate (Goodman, 1996b) and their English miscues demonstrated greater use of effective and efficient reading. They made fewer disruptive miscues, and when they were disruptive, readers usually self-corrected. Through RMA conversations, the teacher and students explored miscues to minimize word-focused skills such as sounding out and looking for little words in big words as examples.

Instead of attacking words, RMA discussions explore how readers use their meaning-making strategies to become more proficient readers. The study resulted in all readers becoming better readers on many different measures and more confidently focusing their attention on comprehension (Goodman & Flurkey, 1996). Additional RMA research with ESL readers provides similar evidence of the success of using RMA with diverse age ranges and populations (Kim, 2010).

Chanho, a highly proficient reader in Korean, was working with a teacher researcher to develop his English literacy. He believed strongly that reading needed to be error-free, believing in the "efficacy of the text." The following miscue is from his reading of the same folktale used with Erica above (Kim, 2010):

Text: When the wife went *into the* house

Chanho: When the wife went *to his . . . into the* house (p. 131)

During the RMA conversation, the teacher explored with Chanho that his self-corrections revealed his knowledge of English grammar, his ability to use English cues and predict prepositional phrases. He agreed that in this case *his* and *the* were synonymous and that his substitutions were grammatically acceptable. When the teacher asked, "do your miscues make sense?," Chanho admitted that they were semantically acceptable in the story but that being accurate was more important in English to understand the author's intent. Chanho thought that every miscue must be corrected.

After 6 RMA sessions, Chanho did agree his Korean reading miscues revealed his understanding and appropriate interpretations of the text based on his knowledge of Korean. He also began to accept that his miscues and self-corrections in reading English demonstrated understanding and that he was capably using grammar and semantic knowledge using evidence from his predictions and correction strategies. He was reading for comprehension, using sampling, predicting, and confirming/disconfirming successfully in reading both in Korean and English.

Chanho slowly began to revalue his strengths in reading English, which resulted in his becoming more proficient. At the same time, he built confidence, which supported him to become more adventurous in reading more complex and diverse materials in English. Discussing miscues in first and second languages provides readers with evidence that effective readers focus on meaning-making. High-quality miscues show that readers are interpreting the text and using background knowledge to predict and confirm (Goodman, Goodman, & Allen, 2016).

Teachers in elementary, middle, and high school use miscue analysis and RMA in their classrooms as part of reading instruction and the ongoing curriculum. Bill Brummet and Lisa Maras (1995) engaged middle-school students in language inquiry through RMA. They discussed with their students how readers' miscues showed their understandings. Students began to value their own miscues, to move away from word-focused views of reading, and became more excited about reading.

The teachers wrote, "Miscue analysis provides a framework for us to make teaching decisions. We realize miscues are crucial. How these are viewed by the child and the teacher determine actions both will take (p. 27)." After they become comfortable with understanding why they make miscues, students often say that their miscues produce language that sounds a lot better than what the author has written.

Heidi Bacon organized her Arizona high school English class that included ESL students to discuss their reading through RMA and as a result shed deficit views of themselves as readers. She involved students daily in self-selected silent reading and lots of writing. Her students became more confident as they discovered that their miscues reflected their grammatical and semantic knowledge and that many of their miscues made sense in context, indicating their ability to predict and confirm based on explicit information in the text. They discussed thoughtfully how they focused on making sense.

Caryl Crowell engaged multiaged second- and third-grade bilingual students in reading conferences using RMA (Crowell, 2015). After completing an English and Spanish miscue analysis for each student, which she did three times a year, she helped students explore their miscues to understand their competencies in each language and how this reflected their search for meaning. She described: "it forever changed the way I listened to readers and thought about my students as readers, as well as the kinds of instructional engagements I offered in my classroom" (pp. 3–4).

"Every reading is a learning experience and contributes to continuous reading development" (Goodman, Martens, & Flurkey, 2016, p. 224). It is important for teachers and students to see how learning experiences and everyday literacy, even in students' first language, support their continued language and literacy development. We must not underestimate the importance of using students' L1 knowledge to support their developing L2 reading.

Language learners develop greater confidence when their languages are valued. When teachers expand learning opportunities and appreciate the multiple languages learners bring to schooling, *language as a resource* is magnified. Readers and teachers come to appreciate that miscues reveal the ways in which readers are constructing meaning and the knowledge it takes to do so.

Involving readers in exploring miscues in their proficient language provides second-language English readers with opportunities to consider the power of being bilingual. Biliterate texts that include both languages are exciting to hear read aloud and to explore the intelligence it takes to shift from Spanish to English phonology appropriately (Krumgold & Charlot, 1953).

Principle 5: Language, Including Reading, Is Learned in the Context of Its Use with Authentic Materials for Personal and Social Purposes.

According to John Dewey, curriculum is everything that happens to the learner in the instructional setting. We believe students learn to read and write best when they are using literacy throughout and engaging and rich curriculum focused on topics of interest meaningful to the students (Cambourne, 1995). Students learn to read and write while reading and writing to learn. Learners develop literacy as they explore concepts and issues in the range of subject matter areas: science, social studies, art, music, math. Whenever students use language, they learn language, learn through language, and learn about language (Halliday, 2003).

An early step in planning curriculum involves the teacher knowing the student in relation to their language and cultural and intellectual resources. Teachers gather data and build profiles that include readers' resources, strengths, and needs by interviewing students and parents. Teachers document learning through kidwatching: taking notes, keeping records (Goodman, 1996a). While students are involved in engaging experiences, the teacher talks with students, inviting them to pose questions and to inquire about what they are most interested in.

Teachers record students' use of L1 and L2, how they interact with others in each language, and their understanding of concepts in various subject matter areas, and document students' emotional responses to each of their languages. As teachers introduce curricular experiences, the contexts they organize relate new language and understandings to what students already know and are comfortable with. As a result, learners come to appreciate that they expand knowledge based on what they already know. And while the students are engaged in learning about their world, teachers help them focus on how they use language to learn.

We use the Burke Reading Interview (BRI) (Goodman, Watson, & Burke, 2005) to provide insights into readers' views of the reading process. Responses to "When you are reading and you come to something the gives you trouble what do you do? Does the best reader you know ever come to something he or she doesn't know? What would he or she do?," and "How would you help a person who was having difficulty?" reveal what the reader believes about reading? "Do you think you are a good reader" and "What would you like to do better as a reader" reveal what the reader thinks about him/herself as a reader.

Readers' emotional responses toward reading influence how they read and their levels of confidence about reading and learning (Allen, 2016; Liwanag, 2006). Understanding readers' perceptions about reading is the beginning of supporting readers in seeing the value of their resources and capabilities.

ESL readers need to appreciate their first language in learning to read their second language. The BRI questions are adapted for ESL and adult readers (http://www.retrospectivemiscue.com). The student's profile keeps expanding as the teacher adds information about the learner's developing concepts throughout the curriculum.

We focus on curricular experiences that teachers develop in relation to second-language learners' interests and questions using authentic materials. Literacy digs help students become consciously aware of how pervasive and diverse literacy use is (Goodman, 2003) when students are invited to research and document what people read and write in the context of their home and community.

Students often believe that there is nothing to read in their homes, but after discussions about medication, cleaning supplies, food labels, clothing labels, logos on sports equipment, directions, cell phones, computers, video games, and the like, the discussion becomes illuminating as learners become aware of how pervasive literacy is in their lives and how much they already know about written language. The political nature of marketing and advertising often becomes an issue during discussions as students become aware of how central literacy is to their daily lives.

Students keep lists of what they read and write from the minute they get up to the time they go to bed. They record what is readable on the streets and in school. Younger children might even take a walk through their neighborhoods to document what written language they see. Students note how different writing events cause learners to shift to their first- or second-language talk and how context influences language use. Lists, diagrams, and pictures of literacy are prominently displayed in classrooms and hallways and added to over time to extend the discussion of literacy as a cultural form in society.

These discussions often focus on when students feel it is appropriate to use which languages and why? Discussions about the "rights" people have to use their own language for learning purposes is another topic some classes often explore, and time is spent on talking about a range of language issues (Goodman, 2003). The growing uses of technology highlight the kinds of literacy learning that have changed over time, as students and the teacher explore literacy through social media, smartphones, tablets, and how oral and written language in English and L1 continue to develop simultaneously.

Kathy Lohse (1998) teaches in a bilingual kindergarten where English and Spanish are used throughout the day. She teaches in "The *Tree* Room," where children explore how humans, animals, and plants grow. Ms. Lohse selects one student weekly to spotlight as a "*tree* mendous person." A letter is sent home to invite family members to collect photos, mementos, and family stories about the "tree mendous" child to share in school. These are added to the large bulletin board tree, which already includes the child's name, stories, drawings, and photos.

Family members are invited to class to read and share stories about the focus child, and they hang related artifacts on the tree. Although presenters are encouraged to use English, if they choose to use their dominant language the child or teacher serves as translator and interpreter. The other children in the class draw and write letters about their views of the child's special contributions, and these are added to the display. Throughout the week, the display is updated, read aloud, and talked about.

Others teachers in lower grades set up shopping centers or kitchen corners next to white boards or play stations. These become centers easily designed by learners and teachers to honor home languages and expand on English at the same time. Students display packages from food items brought from home where children can read cans, cereal boxes, and advertisements in multiple languages.

In a kindergarten in Yaffo in Israel that Yetta visited, there was a corner area with shelves of food boxes and cans in Russian, Arabic, Hebrew, and English. Every child was an expert in one or more of these languages that the foods represented. They put the items they brought from home into the play "store," which they also used for math and geography explorations.

In another first grade, teachers set up a doctor's corner with charts of every child in the class, including both first and second languages as appropriate. The children weighed and measured and kept other notes about each other as relevant to the interests of the children and their understanding of the information doctors need to know about patients. Opportunities are endless for constructing spaces where students collaborate, engage in reading and writing, and share their interest in language.

Upper-elementary and middle-school teachers place large maps on their walls and invite students to find their countries of origin, placing pins and names in appropriate places. They discuss patterns of migrations from one country to another. The class celebrates the experiential diversities about their languages and experiences coming to the United States.

A secondary-school teacher involves her second-language students in producing *Here's Our Weekly News*. She introduces the newspaper's possibilities by displaying many different kinds of newspapers around the room a week or two before she invites a local journalist to speak with the students about how newspapers are planned, organized, published, and distributed.

Students get involved in discussions with the journalist about whether newspapers will disappear and whether news will eventually only be available electronically. The class visits a publishing house and discovers aspects of producing a newspaper, and the students write their own newsletter to share with other students and their families.

The students in some of her classes decided to send their weekly newsletters to their parents to let them know what happens in various classes. Two parents responded in their home languages, not in English. The students then sent another newsletter to parents translating the letters into English. This then became a regular pattern.

There was a section in the newsletter where students and parents were encouraged to ask questions about the lives of classmates from different countries. Parents responded to these questions with stories, poems, songs, cartoons, and drawings. Students encouraged family members to write about schooling experiences in their countries. Translation opportunities, often in small groups, engaged students in expanding their English language learning.

The power of second-language learning is to build and expand on all languages students are learning, as students are encouraged to bring their questions and wonderings to class when they are involved in developing curriculum in response to what they are eager to learn.

CONCLUSIONS AND RECOMMENDATIONS

Revaluing Second-Language Readers/Learners

Learning environments in which multiple languages are honored for instruction and curriculum purposes provide rich opportunities for students to use English and their varied languages to make use of all symbol systems, including art, music, social and physical science, and math, to continuously enrich the curriculum. Organizing with such a classroom context in mind exploits the concept of translanguaging, and learners revalue language, build confidence, and are in control of expanding their own language capabilities, not simply *adding* a second or third language.

In a report for the Ministry of Education in New Zealand, Peters (2010) states:

> Thompson (2002) proposed that children come to school with virtual school bags filled with knowledge, experiences and dispositions. Although in some contexts school only draws on the contents of selected bags, "those whose resources match those required in the game of education" (Thompson & Hall, 2008, p. 89), ideally schools will recognise and celebrate the learning and experiences that all children bring to school (Thompson, 2002), and build on these as a starting point for curriculum development (Broström, 2005; Timperley, McNaughton, Howie, & Robinson, 2003). This helps to develop confidence (Gregory, 2005) and overcome the problems of school being disheartening if children discover what they know, think and find important is not necessarily on the agenda of their teacher. (Brooker, 2008)

The mother and child we introduced at the beginning of this chapter will both benefit from revaluing their language and literacy environment by engaging in conversations that position both of them in seeing Spanish literacy privileged as much as English. Both will also benefit from spending time in a classroom organized like The Tree Room (Lohse, 1998) where the language and culture of each student is celebrated by peers, parents, and teachers and used to further support an exciting curriculum in two or more languages.

Valuing language as a resource positions readers to see the smart things they do (Goodman, 1996b) and prepares them as lifelong learners and competent readers and writers.

REFERENCES

Allen, K. (2016). *Restorying literacy: The role of anomaly in shifting perceptions of college readers*. (Doctoral dissertation). Available from ProQuest Dissertations & Theses Global.

Allen, K., & Goodman, K. (In press). Revaluing reading. In J. Damico & M. Ball (Eds.), *Sage encyclopedia of human communication sciences and disorders*. Thousand Oaks, CA: Sage Publications.

Brummet, B., & Maras, L. (1995). Liberated by miscues: Students and teachers discovering the reading process. *Primary Voices, 3*(4), 23–31.

Cambourne, B. (1995). Towards an educationally relevant theory of literacy learning: Twenty years of inquiry. *The Reading Teacher, 49*(3), 182–192.

Creese, A., & Blackledge, A. (2010). Translanguaging in the bilingual classroom: A pedagogy for learning and teaching? *Modern Language Journal, 94*(1), 103–115.

Crowell, C. (1995). Documenting the strengths of bilingual readers. *Primary Voices, 3*(4), 32–38. Retrieved from http://www.ncte.org/journals/pv/issues/v3-4.

Crowell, C. (2015). Miscue analysis V. DIBELS: A tale of resistance. *Talking Points, 26*(2), 2–9.

Davenport, M. (2002). *Miscues not mistakes: Reading assessment in the classroom*. Portsmouth, NH: Heinemann.

Dworin, J. E. (April 1, 2003). Insights into biliteracy development: Toward a bidirectional theory of bilingual pedagogy. *Journal of Hispanic Higher Education, 2*(2), pp. 171–186.

Edelsky, C. (1991). *With literacy and justice for all: Rethinking the social in language and education*. London: Falmer Press.

Ferreiro, E., & Teberosky, A. (1982). *Literacy before schooling*. Exeter, NH: Heinemann Educational Books.

Freeman, A. (2001). The eyes have it: Oral miscue and eye movement analysis of the reading of fourth grade Spanish/English bilinguals. (Doctoral dissertation). Available from ProQuest Dissertations & Theses Global.

García, O., & Wei, L. (2014). *Translanguaging: Language, bilingualism and education*. London, England: Palgrave Macmillan.

González, N. (2015, December). Imagining literacy equity: *Theorizing flows of community practices*. Plenary Address presented at Literacy Research Association, Carlsbad, CA.

Goodman, K. (1976). Miscues: Windows on the reading process. In K. Goodman (Ed.), *Miscue analysis: Applications to reading instruction* (pp. 3–14). Urbana, IL: ERIC Clearing House on Reading and Communication Skills.

Goodman, K., Fries, P., & Strauss, S. (2016). *Reading the grand illusion: How and why people make sense of print.* New York: Routledge.

Goodman, K., & Goodman, Y. (2014). *Making sense of learners making sense of written language: The selected works of Kenneth S. Goodman & Yetta M. Goodman.* New York: Routledge.

Goodman, K., Goodman, Y., & Allen, K. (2016). Research on helping readers make sense of print: Evolution of comprehension based pedagogy. In S. Israel (Ed.), *Handbook of research on reading comprehension* (Vol. II). New York: Guilford Press.

Goodman, K., Goodman, Y., & Flores, B. (1979). *Reading in the bilingual classroom: Literacy and biliteracy.* Rosslyn, VA: Interamerica.

Goodman, K., Wang, S., Iventosch, M., & Goodman, Y. (2011). *Reading in Asian languages: Making sense of written texts in Chinese, Japanese and Korean.* New York: Routledge.

Goodman, Y. (1990). *How children construct literacy: Piagetian perspectives.* Newark, DE: International Reading Association.

Goodman, Y. (1996a). Kidwatching: An alternative to testing. In S. Wilde (Ed.), *Notes from a kidwatcher: Selected writings of Yetta M. Goodman* (pp. 211–218). Portsmouth, NH: Heinemann.

Goodman, Y. (1996b). Revaluing readers while readers revalue themselves: Retrospective Miscue Analysis. *Reading Teacher, 49*(8), 600–609.

Goodman, Y., & Anders, P. (1999). Listening to Erica read: Perceptions and analyses from six perspectives. In T. Shanahan, F. Rodriguez-Brown, C. Worthman, et al. (Eds.), *The forty-eighth yearbook of National Reading Conference* (pp. 178–198). Chicago, IL: National Reading Conference, Inc.

Goodman, Y., & Flurkey, A. (1996). Retrospective miscue analysis in middle school. In Y. Goodman & A. Marek (Eds.), *Retrospective miscue analysis: Revaluing readers and reading* (pp. 87–105). Katonah, NY: Richard C. Owen Publishers.

Goodman, Y., Martens, A., & Flurkey, P. (2014). *Retrospective miscue analysis: A window into readers' thinking.* Katonah, NY: Richard C. Owen Publishers.

Goodman, Y., Martens, A., & Flurkey, P. (2016). Revaluing readers: Learning from Zachary. *Language Arts, 93*(3), 213–225.

Goodman, Y. M. (2003). *Valuing language study: Inquiry into language for elementary and middle schools.* Urbana, IL: National Council of Teachers of English.

Goodman, Y. M., Watson, D. J., & Burke, C. L. (2005). *Reading miscue inventory: from evaluation to instruction.* Katonah, NY: Richard C. Owen Publishers.

Gregory, E. (2008). *Learning to read in a new language: Making sense of words and worlds.* Thousand Oaks, CA: Sage Publications.

Halliday, M. (2003). Three aspects of children's language development: Learning language, learning through language, learning about language (1980). In J. Webster (Ed.), *The language of early childhood, Volume 4: The collected works of M.A.K. Halliday* (pp. 308–326). London: Continuum.

Kim, M. (2010). *Adult ESL Korean readers' responses about their reading in L1 Korean and L2 English.* (Doctoral dissertation). Available from ProQuest Dissertations and Theses database (UMI No. 3402930).

Krumgold, J., & Charlot, J. (1953). *And now Miguel.* New York: Thomas Y. Crowell.

Liwanag, M. P. S. U. (2006). *Affect in secondary students' reading as revealed by their emotional responses in retrospective miscue analysis.* (Doctoral dissertation). Available from ProQuest Dissertations & Theses Global. (305353120).

Lohse, K. (1998). *Writing letters: Moving from invention to convention in a bilingual kindergarten.* Unpublished Teacher Research Project, University of Arizona.

McInnes, J. (Ed.). (1962). The man who kept house. In *Magic and make believe*. Toronto, Canada: Thomas Nelson and Sons.

Meek, M. M. (1988). *How texts teach what readers learn*. Stroud, Glos: Thimble Press.

Menosky, D. (1971). *A psycholinguistic description of oral reading miscues generated during the reading of varying portions of text by selected readers from grades two, four, six, and eight*. (Doctoral dissertation). Available from ProQuest Dissertations and Theses database (UMI No. 7214600).

Morales, A., & Hanson, W. E. (2005). Language brokering: An integrative review of the literature. *Hispanic Journal of Behavioral Sciences, 27*(4), 471–503.

Orellana, M., & García, O. (2014). Language brokering and translanguaging in school. *Language Arts, 91*(5), 386–392.

Peters, S. (2010). Literature review: Transition from early childhood education to school. Report for the Ministry of Education. Retrieved from: http://www.educationcounts.govt.nz/publications/ECE/98894/Chapter_4.

Ruiz, R. (March 08, 1984). Orientations in language planning. *Nabe: The Journal for the National Association for Bilingual Education, 8*(2), 15–34.

Thomas S., Laccetti J., Mason, B., Mills, S., Perril, S., & Pullinger, K. (2007). Transliteracy: Crossing divides, *First Monday, 12*(2).

Watson, D. (2011). Where do we go from here?: From miscues to strategies. In R. Meyer & K. Whitmore (Eds.), *Reclaiming reading: Teachers, students, and researchers regaining spaces for thinking and action* (pp. 67–77). New York: Taylor & Francis/Routledge.

Whitmore, K. F., Martens, P., Goodman, Y. M., & Owocki, G. (December 1, 2004). Critical lessons from the transactional perspective on early literacy research. *Journal of Early Childhood Literacy, 4*(3), 291–325.

Chapter Five

Language Development in Early Readers and Writers

Carol Owles

In this chapter, the author presents a disposition for teaching and learning that requires practicing teachers to view all learners in today's classrooms as needing to be nurtured, appreciated, and challenged. Students need to be taught in a way that capitalizes on their special talents and gifts, learning modes, and particular needs. Being bilingual or multilingual is one such talent and gift. Key elements of this chapter are classroom practices and instructional approaches that build on children's strengths and incorporate the resources of family and community.

    The views, ideas, thoughts, and research that are presented in the following chapter are based on over two decades of experiences of the author, an early childhood educator. As a teacher of young children, language development and emergent literacy are two important areas to consider when helping students become literate. Add to that the fact that in many classrooms today, there are students whose first language is not English. These English learners (ELs) require much special knowledge and understanding on the part of the teacher. It is very important for teachers to learn more about the accommodations that ELs need in order to be successful.

    All children need to be nurtured, appreciated, and taught in a way that capitalizes on each of his/her special talents, gifts, and learning modes. Their particular needs should also be considered. Being bilingual, trilingual, or multilingual is one such talent and gift of many young children in our classrooms.

In studying the research in this area, the work of Luis Moll has probably had the most influence and impact on this author's thinking, beliefs, and teaching practices. His research also fits this author's personal philosophy of teaching young children. This philosophy includes the belief that each child needs to be appreciated for what he or she brings to the classroom. The strengths of each child are what should be emphasized and built upon, rather than focusing on their lack of skills or the knowledge that they have not yet developed.

This is especially relevant when considering ELs' developing knowledge of English. The language(s) they speak and their knowledge of how to utilize that language to think and communicate their thoughts and ideas are their strengths. Building on those strengths to help them learn English is an effective teaching approach. A fair and equitable stance looks at each learner from an additive stance, rather than noting his or her deficits. Each young learner comes to the classroom with many talents and abilities and much knowledge. Consider the following quote by Emsy Dunn that had a prominent place in the author's kindergarten classroom:

The child is not going TO BE somebody/ He or she IS already somebody.

Moll's work (Au, Carroll, & Scheu, 2001) emphasizes that second-language learners from working-class families and backgrounds receive a different quality of education from that of middle-class students. An EL's education often includes rote instruction, rather than instruction that includes high levels of thinking and conceptual understanding. ELs are frequently given fewer opportunities for choice, as opposed to allowing children to choose what interests them. Choice is a major motivating factor in learning.

The rich content of the curriculum is an important component for all learners, including, and especially, for ELs. Moll (Au, Carroll, & Scheu, 2001) found that the complexity of the curriculum is often reduced or is less rigorous to match the ELs' ability to speak English. Some still view ELs who are learning the intricacies and nuances of the English language as not able to understand or learn major concepts of the curriculum—just because of their lower proficiency levels of English. This ignores the fact that children can and may understand more than they are able to express in English. They may be literate and able to understand in their first or home language, but not able to communicate their understanding or convey their thoughts in English. When teachers fail to acknowledge and recognize this fact, they hamper ELs' academic achievement.

It is important to encourage learners to participate in activities such as requiring that they give their opinions on a topic, research a topic of interest, and read books of their choice. Activities such as these allow young learners to present their understandings in multiple ways. As a result, this enhances the opportunities for children to grow in their understandings and their first and second language abilities. By utilizing such practices as listed above, teachers can work from students' strengths to build on what they already know and what they can already do. These expectations and opportunities are important for all learners, including ELs. This view of how children learn most effectively is an important aspect of teaching practices and the way that educators should view all students. This is particularly important for ELs and students from low-income families.

In many schools today, there are family literacy programs, particularly those that serve low-income families or families who speak a first language other than English, that tend to take a neo-deficit approach. "Despite the discourse on family strengths, many schools still fail to fully recognize, incorporate, or tap into the wealth of information, skills, and knowledge that parents may hold in the area of literacy" (Ortiz & Ordoñez-Jasis, 2005, p. 111). Teachers need to create opportunities for their students to make connections between the academic language of the classroom and their real life experiences.

To accomplish this, Moll reminds us that ELs come from families that possess *funds of knowledge* in fields like agriculture, religion, the arts, and medicine (Moll, 1992; Moll & Gonzáles, 1994). Tapping these funds of knowledge by involving parents/families as resources in our classrooms helps ELs see the connections between their own lives and what they are learning in school. This helps the learners grasp that nontraditional knowledge is as valuable as schooled knowledge (González, Moll, & Amanti, 2005).

Besides utilizing these funds of knowledge, teachers need to provide scaffolds for their students between what they know and learn at home (nonschooled knowledge) and the academic language of the classroom. This academic language is necessary to grasp concepts taught in the content areas and becomes visible to the learners in the read-alouds that teachers use in their teaching.

Many times, families from other cultures and backgrounds are not sure how or what to do to show their interest and commitment to their children's learning. They are also not sure of what is acceptable and expected participation in school activities. The value of acknowledging, utilizing, and celebrating these kinds of contributions is so important to building the confidence and self-esteem of the child, the family, and the community. This, in turn, encourages more participation and learning in school for both the children and their parents.

To be effective teachers for all children, educators can look at the research of Cunningham and Allington and that of Moll for the similarities in their findings on effective teaching. Cunningham and Allington (2007) state that "the most effective teachers emphasize higher-level thinking skills from the beginning. They ask questions that do not have just one answer and engage students in conversations and encourage them to have conversations with one another" (p. 8).

Moll's studies emphasize that effective teachers believe that literacy instruction should center on developing all students' abilities to make meaning, gain understanding, and communicate ideas with others (Au, Carroll, & Scheu, 2001). Cunningham and Allington (2007) state that "exceptional teachers teach skills and strategies and provide lots of time each day for children to read and write. They integrate reading and writing with the content areas" (pp. 7–8).

Moll's view (Au, Carroll, & Scheu, 2001) is that effective teachers involve students in purposeful and meaningful activities involving varied uses of literacy. ELs read and write and do so for a variety of purposes. They should be encouraged to write on topics of their own choice that reflect their own backgrounds and experiences. They need opportunities to write in their first language, as well as opportunities where they are required to use the English language that they are learning. When "the teacher takes into account the interests and needs of the children, the students are more interested in what they are reading and writing" (Cunningham & Allington, 2007, p. 9).

From Moll's work in schools in Tucson, Arizona, he explained, "We believe that a meaning-centered model (of teaching) . . . allows bilingual students to take full advantage of their first language abilities and to surpass the limits set by their more limited knowledge of their second language." He encouraged teachers to look at children as "active learners," using and applying literacy as a tool for communication and thinking.

All three researchers stress the importance of active engagement in classroom activities and lessons. This is based on tapping into the interests, needs, and backgrounds of the children. When children are interested and have choice in what they are studying and learning, their engagement and participation increases. For all students, Moll's *funds of knowledge* can be utilized to enrich the curriculum (Au, Carroll, & Scheu, 2001). When families are involved and teachers demonstrate that they value the contributions that families make to the classroom, it helps create a community of learners, rich in talents, interests, and resources.

Another factor that is similar in the research of effective teaching for all children, including ELs, is the importance of a well-managed classroom. Teachers must expect children to behave, and they need to make these expectations known (Cunningham & Allington, 2007). This is important when helping learners to develop insights into cultural norms that take them outside the confines of their home cultures. Such conditions allow for high levels of engagement for all learners, regardless of their cultures of origin.

EMERGENT LEARNERS' ORAL LANGUAGE: APPLICATIONS FOR THE CLASSROOM

Another important and essential component of effective literacy instruction is the need to help students develop their oral-language capabilities. Oral language is the system in which spoken words are used to express ideas, feelings, and knowledge. To develop emergent learners' oral language, teachers need to help students develop the skills and knowledge that are used in listening and speaking. Lesaux and Harris (2015) remind us that having the words to engage in dialogue (i.e., vocabulary knowledge) is a key part of oral language. This, in turn, is a key part of comprehending in reading and communicating, using print, and in writing (Beck, McKeown, & Kucan, 2013).

As teachers build on children's oral language abilities, they need to include read-alouds for developing young learners' vocabulary and comprehension skills. As teachers read aloud to students, they need to make sure that the children understand the vocabulary in the story in order to understand and learn the concepts included in the text that is read to them. Pictures, realia, and discussions of word meanings can help young ELs understand and utilize the words they are learning. Lessons in the next section include ideas for developing students' vocabularies and their comprehension of select key concepts in the content areas of science and math.

Vocabulary Development in a Lesson on Living Creatures

In early literacy experiences, the focus on vocabulary development is important. For young literacy learners, including ELs, real experiences in the form of field trips, speakers in the classroom, demonstrations, and reading and listening to good literature will provide opportunities for them to develop their vocabularies and knowledge of how language works. In addition, word walls, lots of visuals, and word study with technology and games will expand their vocabularies and their understanding.

For content area learning in science, social studies, math, and other disciplines, it is particularly important that all students understand the academic language of the content. Knowing and understanding key vocabulary is critical to comprehension—the main goal of reading.

In primary grade classrooms, a word wall, word journals, themed word posters and word lists, and lessons about words are all integral parts of the curriculum and the environment. Allowing the children to be part of creating the vocabulary and word-learning environment is an important aspect of a literacy-rich classroom.

Lesson on Living Things

The following lesson is part of a study of living things and the attributes that all living things possess. This focus can be part of the science curriculum in an early childhood classroom.

In preparing this lesson, the teacher begins with a study of snails and collects literature about snails, both fictional and informational texts. As the teacher and students read stories, together and separately, especially in the informational genre, key words from the stories are highlighted and discussed. Some of these words and the discussions about them help inform students about the anatomy of snails, their habitats, the different kinds of snails, what they eat, and ways that they are useful creatures in nature. The students can help make lists of important words about snails, as well as other mollusks, as they read books on this topic.

Create word lists and ask ELs to write the words in their native language. Family members can be resources to help with words in another language. Ask students to choose a word that they can illustrate and put their picture on a card next to the written word. Students can draw a picture or find an illustration in one of their books, a magazine, or on the computer. Each word card on the chart can display the English word, the word in the home language(s) of the students in the class, as well as a picture or illustration of the word. Display this word chart in the science area of the classroom.

These word walls and charts become references for all of the students, as they acquire new knowledge about snails and other living creatures. Use the children's knowledge of snails to prepare for a trip to a local pet store. Before the trip, send a note home to families, asking for information or experiences that family members may have had with snails. Ask if a family member would be willing to share that information with the class. It is important to include parents in the study and to let them know about the field trip and the fact that their child will be buying and bringing home a pet snail.

At the pet store, make arrangements for each student to select and purchase a pet snail. Prior to the trip the students can compile a list of questions to ask the store owner on the care of snails. The children can volunteer to ask the questions, and the list of questions can be a reminder of what the entire class wants to learn.

When returning to school, discuss the things that the class learned, including the answers to their questions about snails. Write a class experience story about the trip and the highlights of it, as related by the children. Read the story periodically throughout the week to remind the children about what they learned, as well as review the vocabulary the children used. Have the children create an environment for their individual snails, name them, and observe them daily for about a week, before the snails are sent home. Give each child a small journal to draw on and encourage that they write observations about the snail.

Continue the study of snails. Read about them, send books home with the children to read with their families, and refer often to the word wall of vocabulary about living creatures and snails that the children helped create. As new words are added to the wall and charts, have ELs contribute the words in their home language. In this way, as the children talk, draw, and write in their journals about the things they are learning, they can use their native language to express their thoughts and ideas.

Learning and knowing the vocabulary helps all of the children feel more confident as they contribute to the class discussions, read and write stories, and expand their learning and understanding of snails and living creatures.

As the children learn the academic language of living creatures and, particularly, snails, provide many scaffolds for their learning. Create vocabulary charts in English and the native languages represented in the classroom. Use pictures to illustrate the vocabulary words and concepts. Provide real-life experiences such as the field trip to the pet supply store and the experience of the students caring for their own living creatures. All of these activities and opportunities help enrich the children's learning in very concrete ways.

As teachers, it is important to remember that effective strategies for ELs are effective strategies for all students. If students succeed, it is because they have the benefit of hands-on opportunities to learn and work together as they develop their academic vocabularies. In this way, teachers ensure success for all of their students.

CONCEPT DEVELOPMENT THROUGH HANDS-ON EXPERIENCES AND CONNECTIONS TO PRIOR KNOWLEDGE

Manipulating and handling concrete objects aids young children to understand, learn, and clarify new concepts. Utilizing realia—using real objects and materials from everyday life that are associated with the concept being introduced—makes learning easier and more effective. For young learners who are also ELs, this is especially helpful. ELs not only experience handling real objects to discover the objects' attributes, but also learn the appropriate vocabulary to describe and explain their understanding.

Lesson on Geometric Shapes

In the following lesson, adapted from an idea in Herrell and Jordan (2011), the goal is for the students to understand the attributes of geometric shapes, especially triangles. Cardboard replicas of the shapes—triangles, circles, squares, and rectangles—are utilized to help the children see, feel, and understand these attributes as they handle each shape and discuss their shape.

In early childhood classrooms, many times students, including ELs, can differentiate the various shapes, but tend to only recognize and name the isosceles triangle as a triangle. The circle, square, and rectangle are easier to differentiate since size and color are the only change factors. To help children learn and understand the attributes of all four shapes and be able to recognize the different three-sided shapes as all triangles, a teacher taught the following lesson on shapes, beginning the lesson by showing the children real objects that most would be able to recognize. In this way, teachers help the ELs connect to their prior knowledge.

For this lesson, bring in apples of different shapes, colors, and sizes. Read several books on apples prior to the lesson, and complete several apple activities. Some examples are to sort apples, make applesauce, and taste-test different varieties of apples. This author recommends using a familiar fruit or vegetable in the lesson.

Begin the lesson by showing the class five different apples, two red and two green, and one yellow. Ask them to tell what these objects are. One child might answer, "They are apples." Ask, "How do you know they are apples? What makes them all apples?" Another child might reply, "They are red and green and yellow, just like the apples that were used to make applesauce" or "They all have stems too. And if we tasted them, they would taste like apples and have apple seeds inside them." Cut open an apple to confirm the children's comments.

Continue the lesson by pointing out the stems and how they connect the fruit to the branch of the tree from which they grow. Cut the five apples, show the seeds inside each, and cut enough small pieces for all to taste. Children may comment on how the apples taste—sweet or sour. Confirm that they are right in that they are all tasting apples. Tell them that even though the apples are different colors and have different shapes and tastes, they all have stems, seeds inside, and all taste like apples.

Show them the yellow apple and ask what it is. When a child responds, "It's an apple too. It's just a different color," confirm that the child's comments are correct. Then, make the transition to the triangles and the different shapes that were presented and discussed earlier.

Show the class several large cardboard triangles—a right angle triangle, an isosceles triangle, and an obtuse triangle. Place them on the board in front of the class and remind the students that they are all triangles. Explain, "They don't look exactly alike, but they all have three sides." Run your finger around each side, count, and confirm that each shape has three sides. Pass around many more triangles of various sizes and shapes—all, of course, with three sides. The children can examine each triangle as it is passed to them, and count the three sides on each as they run their fingers around each side.

Finally, put the children in small groups and introduce a sorting activity. Give each group a packet of the shapes of circles, squares, triangles, and rectangles. The shapes are various sizes and colors. The children first sort the shapes into the categories, even though the shapes in each category are not all the same size and color. Then they place all of the various types of triangles together and categorize them as triangles.

Even though some of the children may only recognize an isosceles triangle as a triangle, they are able to transfer knowledge from the discussion of the apples and understand that just as all apples are not exactly the same, they are still apples. Review the similar attributes that made them all apples. Likewise, even though the color, shape, and size of triangles may not be the same, if they have three sides, they are all triangles.

While connecting to prior knowledge is important for all learners, it is particularly essential for children who are transferring concept knowledge between two languages. They not only need to understand the concept they are learning, but also need the vocabulary and nuances of the language to identify and describe the concept. Having the opportunity to handle real objects and to discover and discuss information with others about those objects helps make learning easier to understand and more effective.

RECOMMENDATIONS FOR ACTION

As this educator worked with ELs in a preschool/primary classroom and talked with other teachers, she created a list of teaching ideas and techniques. Recommendations were compiled by this author and through collaboration with two teachers of ELs, S. Bafna and C. O'Dea. These ideas will help you to shape the most optimum learning environment in your classroom and provide effective instruction for young learners, including ELs from diverse backgrounds.

- When thinking about and creating the learning environment in the classroom, it is important to consider what many researchers have proposed. ELs acquire their second language naturally, just like they developed their first languages. Language is acquired in natural settings, such as the classrooms, when students receive lots of comprehensible input. Provide learners opportunities during the day to practice and use their new language in this natural and safe learning environment. As they participate in language experiences, their knowledge of the second language grows.
- Create a print- and language-rich environment. In this way, children will see many examples of the printed word in all of the languages represented in a particular classroom.
- Create a classroom that is a warm, inviting place where all children are welcomed and diversity is valued.
- Get to know your students and their families. Build positive relationships with each student and family and tap into their *funds of knowledge* (Moll, 1992; and Moll & González, 1994, as cited in Au, Carroll, & Scheu, 2001,

p. 18). Utilize the families' talents and contributions to enrich your teaching and the curriculum, as well as the students' learning.
- Sing a lot, laugh a lot, and play games! All of these things are important to ensure ELs' comfort and their feelings of security in the classroom. Small things make a difference in helping ELs adapt to the classroom culture and foster their willingness to participate in learning activities and lessons.
- Involve emergent learners in literacy activities in the very beginning of the school year. Written language remains more constant and is not as fleeting as oral language can be. Use read-alouds or the listening center, so children can follow along as they listen to stories. This will help them make connections between the print and the language that they are acquiring.
- Allow and encourage ELs to use various ways to show their understanding. Gestures, drawings, writing, drama, or oral presentations in English or their native language are all ways to show their ideas and their thinking. Also, be sure to continually check for comprehension/understanding.
- Plan for lots of cooperative work. If possible, put ELs with partners who speak their native language, as well as fluent English. Allow ELs to use their native language in this group work.
- Utilize visuals in your teaching. Maps, models, realia, videos, the smart board, iPads, and hands-on activities offer multimodal input that aids understanding.
- When teaching and explaining concepts, enrich the language that is utilized through repetition, rephrasing, and giving examples. In addition, allow more wait time when asking questions of ELs. This allows time for them to process the question and their answer, as they transfer their knowledge between languages.
- Utilize a variety of assessments. Use ongoing, integrated, multiple, and alternative modes of assessing students' learning, including their oral language, writing, illustrations, and drama. Also, encourage self-assessment.
- Finally, provide opportunities for children to succeed in the work expected of them. Success promotes a healthy, positive self-concept for the learner. This, in turn, makes learners risk-takers who are willing to try new ideas and learning opportunities.

RESOURCES FOR THE CLASSROOM

The following technology applications, websites, and other resources are helpful when working with young ELs.

- Flocabulary.com: This website offers many mini-games to play with vocabulary words that the children are learning. They are fun, interesting, and include ideas for modifying the games for ELs. https://www.flocabulary.com/vocabulary-mini-games/.
- Greene, R. (2013). 5 Key Strategies For ELL Instruction. Retrieved May 10, 2016, from https://www.teachingchannel.org/blog/2013/10/25/strategies-for-ell-instruction/.
- Futaba: Website by INKids Education LLC that offers free downloads in iTunes of lots of word games for children. https://itunes.apple.com/us/app/word-games-for-kids-futaba/id426517722?mt=8.
- Herrell, A., & M. Jordan. (2011). *Fifty strategies for teaching English language learners*, 4th ed. Upper Saddle River, NJ: Pearson Education, Inc.
- PBSkids.org: PBS Kids characters introduce vocabulary games on this website for sorting words, letter recognition, spelling words, and more. http://pbskids.org/games/vocabulary/.
- WE *are* TEACHERS: This website has many vocabulary games. Most are for older students, but the following two are for younger learners: Bingo Vocabulary Games and Color Your Vocabulary Activity http://www.weareteachers.com/blogs/post/2015/01/15/11-vocab-review-games-to-make-the-learning-stick. This website also has articles, printables, vocabulary-building ideas, and teaching tips for working with your English Learners http://www.weareteachers.com/lessons-resources/ell-success.
- Vocabulary.co.il.com: This site has many free downloads for vocabulary and word recognition games for a variety of ages. http://www.vocabulary.co.il/foreign-language/english-word-recognition-game/.

REFERENCES

Au, K., Carroll, J., & Scheu, J. (2001). *Balanced literacy instruction: A teacher resource book*. Norwood, MA: Christopher-Gordon Publishers, Inc.

Bafna, S. (2016). Personal interview.

Beck, I. L., McKeown, M. G., & Kucan, L. (2013). *Bringing words to life: Robust vocabulary instruction*, 2nd ed. New York: Guilford Press.

Cunningham, P. M., & Allington, R. L. (2007). *Classroom that work: They can all read and write*, 4th ed. Boston, MA: Pearson Education.

Funds of Knowledge – A look at Luis Moll's research into hidden family resources. (n.d.). Retrieved May 1, 2016, from https://edsource.org/wp-content/uploads/old/Luis_Moll_Hidden_Family_Resources.pdf.

González, N., Moll, L., & Amanti, C. (Eds.). (2005). *Funds of knowledge for teaching in Latino households*. Mahwah, NJ: Lawrence Erlbaum.

Herrell, A., & Jordan, M. (2011). *Fifty strategies for teaching English language learners*, 4th ed. Upper Saddle River, NJ: Pearson Education.

Lesaux, N. K., & Harris, J. R. (2015). *Cultivating knowledge, building language: Literacy instruction for English learners in elementary school*. Portsmouth, NH: Heinemann.

Moll, L. (1992). Bilingual classroom studies and community analysis. *Educational Researcher, 21*(2), 20–24.

Moll, L. C., & González, N. (1994). Critical issues: Lessons from research with language-minorities children. *Journal of Literacy Research, 26*(4), 429–456.

O'Dea, C. (2002). Personal communication through shared Teaching Notes.

Ortiz, R. W., & Ordoñez-Jasis, R. (2005). Leyendo juntos (reading together): New directions for Latino parents' early literacy involvement. *The Reading Teacher, 59*, 110–121.

Chapter Six

Exploring English Learners' Languages and Cultures through Visual Literacy

Mayra C. Daniel

In memory of Chris Liska Carger

There are numerous ways for teachers to support and acknowledge learners' bilingual-bicultural identities. Socioculturally appropriate instruction creates bridges between linguistic and culturally diverse learners and other members of the school community. Incorporating visual thinking strategies into lessons is an easily implementable pedagogy that will scaffold bilingual learners' understandings of the curriculum, promote additive language development, and encourage multicultural awareness in the schoolhouse.

Chris Liska Carger believed that teaching is a career that involves the heart and the soul of the teacher, the students, their families, and every stakeholder's community and country of origin. She believed teachers are professionals but that most of all, they are individuals committed to ensuring society provides equitable paradigms for living and learning that support the rights of all students to be participants and contributors to the world.

Chris introduced future teachers to the beauty of literature that represents cultural groups around the world when she took teacher candidates to volunteer at schools with populations of English learners (ELs). Her elementary education students participated in a structured course that joined the topics of culture, art, and literature to promote literacy.

In her course, classrooms of K–3rd grade elementary students completed art activities that were linked to the message in the picture books they read with their teacher and the college interns. Activities focused on English vocabulary development within translingual spaces (García & Wei, 2014).

The ELs were asked to read books written in both English and Spanish to meet several goals in each lesson. These were to expose them to unfamiliar English vocabulary, provide them opportunities to use the new language in useful ways, and supply the multimodal input of the visuals present in storybooks. This program, Reaching out through Art and Reading, included an emphasis on visual thinking strategies (VTS) (Housen, 2001–2002).

One of the interns who participated in this program summarized the value of VST in the curriculum as she saw it in practice (C. Chang, personal communication, October 3, 2016). "Students loved the read-alouds! The beautiful illustrations in the books helped to draw them into the story. I saw students learning the vocabulary without noticing. When we developed critical questions for the students, it seemed to help them think and understand the stories."

Before her passing, Chris had begun to explore what she wanted to share in this chapter. Not knowing the exact direction in which she planned to take the reader, this author is making the assumption that she can step in and discuss the contribution of art and VTS to biliteracy both from her point of view and her colleagues'.

STRATEGIC EDUCATORS

All learners succeed when educators are free to investigate, acknowledge, and support their students' *funds of knowledge* (González, Moll, & Amanti, 2005). ELs, whether born in the United States or in a far-off continent of the world, bring experiences to the U.S. schoolhouse that are unique to their families and circumstances. Schooling culturally and linguistically diverse students requires not delivering a one-size-fits-all curriculum.

Students learn from their teachers and it is important that teachers keep in mind that learners are not the only ones who acquire knowledge in the schoolhouse. Educators will also widen their cultural understandings by exploring their students' histories and their communities of origin before and after immigration. Teachers are ethnographers, observers, and interpreters of interpersonal interactions every minute of their day.

Educators' ongoing engagement with students is what results in equitable school communities, where its members respect each other. Competent teachers are satisfied with their work only when they devote sufficient time to understand what their students need them to offer in order to see themselves reflected in the school curriculum.

Instructional paradigms that include a strong component of visual literacy (that reflects the familiar and the unfamiliar) help teachers validate ELs' realities. Housen's research (2001–2002) on a VTS-based curriculum and the development and transfer of critical thinking skills suggests that learners transfer information learned through VTS across social contexts and that this knowledge is transferred first across contexts and then across content.

Educators know that verbal literacy has traditionally been more respected than visual literacy (Arnheim, 2004). However, visual literacy has much to offer, particularly in the 21st century when visual images are more and more prevalent and accessible using current technologies.

Learners today are used to recording events with their cellular phones and sharing this information in text messages that involve reading, writing, and forwarding images across small and distant spaces. Therefore, we can see that visual literacy is a skill that children have already begun to develop when they begin their schooling. Educators need to consider the possibility that all students, even those who do not have the most recent technology at home, have developed learning styles that are visually oriented to a world of Internet communication.

A multiliteracies philosophy values all forms of literacy (Luke, 2003). It acknowledges that there is a need for learners to read, interpret, understand, and create visual communications strategically. The technologies that we use as part and parcel of our daily lives in 2017 join visual and verbal literacy because they engage students in multimodal instruction that includes the ongoing juncture of visual images, written text, music, and interactive tasks (Daniel & Shin, 2015; Gangwer, 2009).

COMMON CORE: ENGLISH LANGUAGE ARTS

For those teachers concerned with their district's requirements for integration of the Common Core State Standards, know that visual literacy appears in the English Language Arts section (Common Core State Standards Initiative, 2010). Once students develop the ability to use visual literacy strategies in the language arts, they are able to apply them in all content areas to engage all modalities of expression.

Visual literacy becomes the medium to ask questions, which leads to reflection and critical analyses of text. As students explore what they do not understand, they do so within a nonthreatening environment. With teacher encouragement, ELs have opportunities to develop English and master the art of arguing for or against an idea. Images lend themselves to multiple interpretations, even when there are words attached to the visual that might sway a reader's opinions. Authentic images do not provide only one answer or limit interpretations to the artist's single perspective.

BENEFITS OF USING VISUAL THINKING STRATEGIES

Talking about art is typically relegated to museum educators and art teachers, but this should not be the norm. Discussions about art can afford many benefits to ELs as well. In the aesthetic domain, visual literacy includes being able to interpret and discuss the significance of art. In the context of schools, the ability to interpret visual information and to use it to grasp content must be recognized as essential to reaching academic success across all disciplines. Students can learn to talk about art just as they can learn to talk about literature. They can do so right in the language arts class, in the science, math, and foods class, and so on.

Viewing a work of art and sharing reactions to it provides the opportunity to authentically engage in conversation. Responding to art and other types of images can enable rich interpersonal interactions for ELs to safely experiment and develop language, observational skills, and critical thinking. Many works of art tell a story that can gain students greater access to content area topics as narrative discourse evolves.

Art often expresses cultural values and beliefs. If carefully selected, ELs may connect with cultural expressions visible in art. *Reading* a picture encourages multiple perspectives and gives students who struggle with decoding in a first or a second language a moment to shine using VTS.

Art's Contribution to Social and Emotional Development

A 2016 report by the Committee for Children (retrieved from cfchildren.org, 2016) highlights five interrelated competencies that educators should strive to develop in learners. These consider cognitive, affective, and behavioral development. These competencies address the learner's ability in the areas of (1) self-awareness, (2) self-management, (3) social awareness, (4) relationship skills, and (5) responsible decision-making.

Teacher awareness that social and emotional learning (SEL) and development touches all areas of the learner's identity suggests a need to explore the reasons VTS might contribute to the learner's sense of self and positive self-esteem. Data from a national teacher survey conducted by Civic Enterprises focused on SEL supports what many educators assume. This is that "Poor student behavior is a bigger problem in schools with a *limited focus on SEL*" (Bridgeland, Bruce, & Hariharan, 2013, p. 6).

Instruction that incorporates visual strategies certainly appears to be an avenue to empower students to learn to examine their ideas and learn to express these ideas effectively (Durlak, Taylor, Weissberg, & Schellinger, 2011; Yenawine, 1999). Vygotsky (2002) encouraged teachers to dialogue and engage learners in critical consciousness. He described the competent educator as "no longer being the-one-who-teaches, but one who is himself taught in dialogue with the students" (p. 80). Vygotsky would likely support the use of VTS because this pedagogy provides ELs opportunities to develop and express their voice.

Art's Contribution to Biliteracy and Bicultural Identity Development

Art can increase ELs' comprehension (Dunn & Finley, 2010) and long-term retention of information because visual images add a dimension to the learning (Rinne, Gregory, Yarmolinskaya, & Hardiman, 2011; Daniel & Parada, 2008). Guzetti (2012) discussed the interdisciplinary nature of the visual arts and their contribution to "practical classroom applications" (p. 666). Teachers can select books with images that represent the cultures of all the learners in a classroom and thus validate and support their emergent multicultural identities. "One way to encounter another culture is to observe and discuss the artwork from that culture and a student's own culture" (Daniel & Huizenga-Mc Coy, 2014, p. 173). Authentic art selections for ELs of varied backgrounds will provide avenues that increase the number of bridges to comprehension available to the students (Rufo, 2011; de Jong & Harper, 2005; John-Steiner, 1995). Pathways that link images to language expression make it possible for individuals to rejoice in "our differences and our similarities, because together they are what make us all human" (Bishop, 1990, p. x).

Images of characters that represent real people in the students' communities are key to the sharing of culturally conscious ideologies (McNair, 2010; Yoon, Simpson, & Haag, 2010). ELs need to feel safe contributing to classroom tasks while in the process of acquiring English. ELs from all backgrounds can write and illustrate their own stories using their home language and English (Cummins & Early, 2011) in multilingual-multicultural classrooms. When ELs share their stories with each other, they expand their cultural repertoires.

Cummins and Early (2011) documented that writing identity texts is an effective pedagogical practice that helps ELs explore their plurilingual, pluricultural identities. Identity texts also allow parents to see concrete examples of their child's progress and, in their construction, assist the ELs to face and overcome issues of cultural mismatch (Cummins, 2009).

Selecting Artwork That Engages the Learners

It is important to identify and employ guidelines to select culturally appropriate art that will help ELs develop visual and linguistic literacies. First and foremost, developmentally appropriate art subjects should be considered depending on the learners' ages and experiential backpack. For some ELs, it may be necessary to avoid subjects such as war and sexuality, as well as images of the subconscious (Yenawine, 2003). For students beginning to explore VTS, the art that teachers use should be accessible, realistic, and contain family settings, people, and relatable experiences.

Realistic art is more comprehensible for beginner ELs than abstract, complex art. Accessible art has images that are easily understood and connect to students' background knowledge. This is of the utmost importance when working with ELs who may not have had much exposure to works of art and whose background knowledge may differ from mainstream students'.

ELs who are already struggling with verbal literacy need to be able to make sense of the visual images their teachers are presenting to them. They need to feel comfortable enough to share their ideas in their nonnative language. It helps the students to be able to understand and link their worlds to the images on their own without using words in a second language. When this is the case, the ELs can begin their work without teacher facilitation. Although ELs are as curious as any other students, familiar settings, people, and common experiences offer ELs a strong personal link to artistic works.

Teachers will help their ELs self-monitor their use of VTS by teaching students to pose questions when they examine art. Establishing familiarity with initial questions that fit the age of the learners gives students the strategies they need to use images effectively to scaffold their thinking. The following questions will help young students explore images. The language in these questions can be modified for older ELs:

- When I look at this image, what is the first thing that I see?
- What in this image reminds me of my home and neighborhood?
- Do I see faces and people that look like my family members?
- Is there anything that I see in this image that I don't understand?

Engaging Young Students with Multicultural Children's Literature

There is a wealth of beautiful images within children's literature available that can be used right in the classroom. Art "can provide a cognitive introduction to complex content and reinforce ideas that are difficult to express in words" (Daniel & Huizenga-McCoy, 2014, p. 172). Illustrations found in children's literature also include cultural links and reflect learners' diverse funds of knowledge.

Books Depicting Diverse Cultural Practices

Angela Dominguez's *María Had a Little Llamita* (2007) provides Peruvian-inspired settings, clothing, and animals from Peru to young readers. Any one of her watercolor illustrations can spark conversation, especially for rural immigrant students. Francisco Alarcón's seasonal books are also filled with images containing cultural details and familiar people and objects for Mexican students.

Using these authors' illustrations can make a classroom of ELs explode with conversation, reminiscing about experiences in their homeland and those that reflect their families' current situation. In a classroom of ELs of Latino heritage, one of the author's students even noticed the shoes the grandmother wore in one of Carmen Lomas Garza's books and exclaimed, "You see those shoes, *maestro*? Every *abuela* in Mexico wears shoes like them!"

The art of Garza's books reflects her Mexican heritage and experiences she had with her family and in the border towns in the Southwest region of the United States. In the pages of the book *Family Pictures / Cuadros de familia* (2005), Garza depicts a family playing *lotería*, a game similar to bingo that many children of Mexican origin play. Beginning with the cover of this bilingual book, the reader sees how this family comes together and introduces young children to its cultural traditions and family routines.

Demi, in the folktale *The Empty Pot* (1990), helps the reader learn about Chinese culture and values. This book is useful to teach about the geographical features of China. In addition, its main character, Ping, is an admirable character. He exemplifies honesty and strength in the face of disappointment. This book is a wonderful resource to explore perceptions of personal integrity in the Chinese heritage.

What do we see in the illustrations of Pat Mora's haiku poetry book, *Yum! Mmmm! Qué Rico! America's Sproutings*? Through Rafael López's stunning and bright images of fruits and roots, the reader will see foods that come alive as words linked to the colors of nature reflect the life of a culture through its cuisine.

Hena Khan uses colors from Middle Eastern cultures to present components of the Middle East in her book *Golden Domes and Silver Lanterns* (2012). For young children from this part of the world, this book's beautiful and accurate visuals recognize and validate their religious observances and their families' customs.

Award Winning Books

On their website, the American Library Association (www.ala.org) recognizes the exceptional work of authors and illustrators who have received prestigious awards such as the Pura Belpré, the Caldecott, the Batchelder, the Theodor Seuss Geisel, and many others. Some of these awards recognize both the narrative quality in the writing and the book illustrations.

The quality of the illustrations in the books referenced below earned the illustrators selection by award committees. As you select books, remember the diversity present in your school and classroom population. Choose books that represent all students and that also allow you to introduce the learners to the cultures of classmates from other backgrounds. For example, if you teach in a school district whose student populations represent a high percentage of ELs of only one or two ethnicities, examine the diversity within these groups. Then, work to add to the learners' cultural capital by introducing them to other ways of being by using award-winning books.

The Pura Belpré Award recognizes outstanding work on the part of a Latino/a writer and illustrator. It is given in memory of the first children's librarian, storyteller, and author in New York City whose work centered on valuing Puerto Rican folklore. The following books and the illustrators of these books have received either the recognition of receiving the Pura Belpré *medal* or been named to the *honored book* category for their illustrations.

Medal Winners of the Pura Belpré Award (2010–2016)

Engle, M. (2015). *Dream Girl*. Boston, MA: Houghton Mifflin Harcourt.
Morales, Y. (2014). *Viva Frida*. New York: Roaring Brook Press.
Morales, Y. (2013). *Niño Wrestles the World*. New York: Roaring Brook Press.
Schmidt, G. D. (2012). *Martín de Porres: The Rose in the Desert*. Boston, MA: Houghton Mifflin Harcourt.
Tonatiuh, D. (2013). *Diego Rivera: His World and Ours*. New York: Abrams Books for Young Readers.
Velasquez, E. (2010). *Grandma's Gift*. New York: Walker Publishing.
Mora, P. (2009). *Book Fiesta!: Celebrate Children's Day/Book Day: Celebremos El día de los niños/El día de los libros*. New York: Rayo.

Honor Books of the Pura Belpré Award (2010–2016)

Rivera, R. C. (2015). *My Tata's Remedies*. El Paso, TX: Cinco Puntos Press.
Medina, M. (2015). *Mango, Abuela, and Me*. Somerville, MA: Candlewick Press.
Tonatiuh, D. (2015). *Funny Bones: Posada and His Day of the Dead Calavera*. New York: Abrams Books for Young Readers.
Middleton, S. (2014). *Little Roja Riding Hood*. New York: G. P. Putnam's Sons.
Thong, R. G. (2014). *Green Is a Chile Pepper*. San Francisco, CA: Chronicle Books.
Tonatiuh, D. (2014). *Separate Is Never Equal: Sylvia Mendez & Her Family's Fight for Desegregation*. New York: Abrams Books for Young Readers.
Dominguez, A. (2007). *Maria Had a Little Llama / María Tenía una Llamita*. New York: Henry Holt.
Brown, M. (2013). *Tito Puente: Mambo King / Rey del Mambo*. New York: Rayo.
Tonatiuh, D. (2013). *Pancho Rabbit and the Coyote: A Migrant's Tale*. New York: Abrams Books for Young Readers.
Vamos, S. R. (2013). *The Cazuela That the Farm Maiden Stirred*. Watermann, MA: Charlesbridge.
Brown, M. (2011). *Marisol McDonald Doesn't Match /Marisol McDonald No Combina*. New York: Lee and Low Books.

Tafolla, C. (2010). *Fiesta Babies*. New York: Crown Publishing Group.

Novesky, A. (2010). *Me, Frida*. New York: Abrams Books for Young Readers.

Tonatiuh, D. (2010). *Dear Primo: A Letter to My Cousin*. New York: Abrams Books for Young Readers.

The Mildred L. Batchelder Award is awarded to a U.S. publisher for a children's book considered to be the most outstanding of books originally published in a foreign language for the year in a foreign country, later translated into English and published in this country. The following section lists the winners of this award for 2016.

2016 Batchelder Award Winner

- Almagna, B. (2015). *The Wonderful Fluffy Little Squishy*. Brooklyn, NY: Enchanted Lion Books.

2016 Batchelder Honor Books

- Appelfeld, A. (2015). *Adam and Thomas*. New York: Seven Stories Press.
- Suzhen, F. (2014). *Grandma Lives in a Perfume Village*. New York: North South Books.
- Liniers, R. (2015). *Written and Drawn by Henrietta*. New York: TOON Books.

The Caldecott Medal is an award given yearly to the illustrator of the most distinguished American picture book for children (Refer to the list below for 2016 winners). Caldecott books will expose ELs to understandings of their classmates' cultures and to the evolving multicultural worlds of students whose families immigrated to the United States before they did.

Caldecott Medal Awardee 2016

- Mattick, L. (2015). *Finding Winnie: The True Story of the World's Most Famous Bear*. New York: Little, Brown.

Caldecott Honor Books 2016

- Andrews, T. (2015). *Trombone Shorty*. New York: Abrams Books for Young Readers.
- Boston, C. (2015). *Voice of Freedom: Fannie Lou Hamer, Spirit of the Civil Rights Movement*. Somerville, MA: Candlewick Press.
- Henkes, K. (2015). *Waiting*. New York: Greenwillow Books (also a Seuss Honor Book).
- De la Peña, M. (2015). *Last Stop on Market St*. New York: G. P. Putnam's Sons.

The Theodor Seuss Geisel Award honors the authors and illustrators of the most distinguished book for beginning readers published in the United States the prior year. Seuss's books captivate ELs perhaps because of the energy that is visible in their images and the engaging ways that he used English. His books take the ELs past their self-consciousness when faced with unfamiliar words and phrases. The winners of the Seuss awards for 2016 are listed below.

2016 Seuss Medal Winner

- Adler, D. (2015). *Don't Throw It to Mo*. New York: Penguin Young Readers.

2016 Seuss Honor Books

- Fenske, J. (2015). *A Pig, a Fox, and a Box*. New York: Penguin Young Readers.
- Savage, S. (2015). *Supertruck*. New York: Roaring Book Press.

In my time working as a bilingual and English as a second language teacher at levels K–12, I found that my ELs enjoyed reading the whimsically illustrated Dr. Seuss book *Oh Say Can You Say?* (1979). This book did not offer the students a deep philosophical message nor did it relate to my ELs' prior experiences. What this book effectively does for literate ELs who are familiar with the Roman alphabet is provide them an opportunity to play with the sounds of English. I repeatedly observed students lose their inhibitions as they worked to be able to read Seuss's words quickly. The students would ask if they could copy the words and tell me they wanted to memorize the tongue twisters. When my high school students used this book, they would laugh yet trudge through reading the nonsense words. For example, it is hard for students to resist Seuss's words in the beautifully illustrated images of the green beasts sporting purple hair sitting on their tiny island in the tongue twister *West Beast East Beach*. Seuss tells us that, "Upon an island hard to reach, the East Beast sits upon his beach. Upon the West Beach sits the West Beast. Each beast thinks he's the best beast." Seuss's legacy of words and illustrations is impossible to beat when a teacher wishes to be playful!

FACILITATING VISUAL LITERACY

Adapting recommendations for selecting images (VST, 2011) for classrooms with ELs includes ensuring the appropriateness of the art and image for the learners' histories and cultural backgrounds. Ask yourself if the image presents a topic that will be accessible to the students, if it lends itself to multiple interpretations by ELs with different background experiences, if it can be used to create individual stories, and if it reflects the nation's increasing diversity.

Housen and Yenawine (2016) offer a process to begin the development of VTS with students. There are three basic questions that the facilitator asks in VTS:

1. What do you see in this picture? (observational skills)
2. What do you see that makes you say that? (evidentiary reasoning)
3. What else do you see or what more can you find? (layers of meaning)

Older ELs can progress to more complex questions. The teacher has to listen carefully and paraphrase students' comments to acknowledge them and to be sure the entire group hears and comprehends. ELs' efforts to participate should always be honored. This can be done verbally, with gestures, or through facial expressions. Be careful not to share your personal interpretation of the images under discussion because this could leave students with the impression that there is just one right interpretation or that their opinions are not valued.

When a teacher uses art to teach students to use VTS, the process places the educator in the position of the researcher. As the teacher observes classroom interactions and documents how students develop their thoughts, new ideas for lessons will surface. Housen and Yenawine (2016) provide guidelines to evaluate students after they use VTS in lessons. These include jotting down the following components:

- Noting surprising comments from students
- Keeping track of how discussions evolve in the classroom
- Comparing instruction based on VTS with other approaches
- Looking for evidence that VTS use transfers to other courses
- Students' self-monitoring emerging questions
- Observing uses of VTS in the classroom
- Documenting colleagues' questions related to VTS

Be cognizant that art addresses issues that reflect the human experience that may not change across time, while disciplinary texts such as a timeline in history will remain static. Nevertheless, even though art images differ from those in textbooks, it is worthwhile to explore images in content specific books for meaning (see list below). Both types of visuals contribute to learning and will help students make meaning.

Using VTS in the Content Areas

- **Timelines in history class.** Timelines are visuals that are often difficult to interpret. Ask your students to select 2 to 3 points in the timeline that they can link to a visual image in their minds. Have the ELs develop their own illustrated timeline.
- **Visuals in mathematics texts.** Often math problems have images linked to them. These may or may not help the ELs understand what is being asked. Ask the students if and how the image supports the narrative. If they share that the image does not help them understand, have them draw the image they feel would fit better.
- **Images of people.** Images can serve to examine character development in the narratives students read. They situate events within time periods using the dress, hairstyles, and the like in the drawings.
- **Diagrams of scientific processes and phenomena.** Science textbook authors usually include diagrams that use little language, using the few words to identify parts of the diagrams. Have the ELs examine the diagrams in their textbooks and develop their own using the language/languages that they feel gains them greater access to the topic.

One difference between art and textbook images is that art always allows multiple interpretations while images in textbooks may only present one correct answer to a question. In a history text, depending on the country of publication, one would find the description of an event that led to a war leaves little room for new explanations. Similarly, explanations in science texts are assumed to present proven facts that cannot be questioned. For example, until the mid-2000s, all students, regardless of their grade level, were taught that Pluto was the ninth planet in the solar system and that it was the farthest distance from the sun of all the planets. Learners now learn a different fact: Pluto is not a planet but a dwarf planet.

CONCLUSIONS AND RECOMMENDATIONS

This exploration of a VTS-infused curriculum suggests that visual literacy is under-explored and under-appreciated in the schoolhouse. The power of visual representations to give all learners, and especially ELs, access to content, culture, and the development of ideas, both at school and after school, needs to be acknowledged (Jarvis, 2011; Siegel & Panofsky, 2009; Yenawine, 2005).

Educators need to hold more educational conversations with colleagues that cross disciplinary boundaries. These should focus on the benefits of thoughtful and compelling multimodal instruction using VTS. Teachers need to support each other's ingenuity in lesson planning when it comes to including nontraditional vehicles for thinking.

There are lessons to be learned and more research needed about how ELs process additional languages and also learn new disciplinary concepts without having attained high levels of proficiency in the second language. Although the literature is replete with suggestions that assist students to self-monitor their progress such as pre, during, and after reading instruction using graphic organizers, students do not always grasp the powerful link between the use of collaborative image analyses and achieving higher levels of comprehension (Daniel & Parada, 2008).

Teachers' conversations also need to include an examination of how current technologies contribute to learning. Instruction is enhanced with technology's contributions because these address learners' cross-cultural learning styles, deliver content through all modalities, and help ELs process language and ideas.

As you proceed to design lessons for classrooms with ELs remember to:

1. *Review award winning books each year.* Allow the experts to help you. Consult the website of the American Library Association (www.ala.org) before adding to your classroom library. Remember that what you cannot afford to purchase for your classroom, perhaps the school librarian's budget will allow be added to the school's library holdings. Librarians always know which books win the awards for narratives and illustrations each year. Make the argument with school administrators that books selected for their illustrations will help the ELs process meaning as they develop their languages. In addition to the awards discussed previously in this chapter, explore the following: Odyssey Award for Excellence in Audiobooks Production (awarded to recognize the *best audiobook for children or young adults* produced in the United States), Andrew Carnegie Medal (awarded for the most outstanding *video for children*), and Robert F. Sibert Informational Book Medal (awarded for *distinguished writing and illustrations in an informational book* published in the United States).
2. *Teach your ELs to be book critics.* Show them how to complete a review of a book. This will elicit their opinions and inform them that you value their ideas. Ask students to go beyond a book report as they evaluate and judge the work of talented and well-known authors.
3. *Use electronic books.* These cost less. Look into technology grants that will finance books on Kindle, iPads, and other devices.
4. *Trust your instincts.* Remember that the anecdotal notes you write as your ELs complete tasks in your classroom will be useful to further explain achievement test results.
5. *Find ways to finance museum visits.* Work to plan outings with the art teacher in your school. It is easy to overlook the value of inspirational trips when striving to meet standards. Plan museum trips and invite parents to be chaperones.

CHILDREN'S BOOKS CITED

Demi (1990). *The empty pot.* New York: Henry Holt.
Dominguez, A. (2007). *María had a little llamita.* New York: Henry Holt.
Garza, C. L. (2005). *Family pictures / Cuadros de familia.* 15th Anniversary Edition. New York: Lee & Low.
Khan, H. (2012). *Golden domes and silver lanterns.* San Francisco, CA: Chronicle Books.
Mora, P. (2007). *Yum! Mmmm! Qué rico! America's sproutings.* New York: Lee & Low.
Seuss Enterprises. (1979). *Oh say can you say?* New York: Random House.

REFERENCES

Arnheim, R. (2004). *Visual thinking*. (Paperback Edition). Berkeley, CA: University of California Press.

Bishop, R. S. (1990). Mirrors, windows, and sliding glass doors. *Perspectives: Choosing and Using Books for the Classroom, 6*(3), ix–xi.

Bridgeland, J., Bruce, M., & Hariharan, A. (2013). The missing piece: A national teacher survey of how emotional and social learning can empower children and transform schools. Civic Enterprises and Peter D. Hart Research Associates. *Collaborative for Academic, Social, and Emotional Learning,* 1–60.

Committee for Children. (2016). How social-emotional learning helps children succeed in schools, the workplace, and life. Retrieved from www.cfchildren.org.

Change, C. (2016). Personal communication, October 3.

Common Core State Standards. (2010). Common Core State Standards for English Language Arts & Literacy in History / Social Studies, Science, and Technical Subjects. Retrieved from www.corestandards.org.

Cummins, J. (2009). Pedagogies of choice: Challenging coercive relations of power in classrooms and communities. *International Journal of Bilingual Education and Bilingualism, 2*(3), 261–271.

Cummins, J., & Early, M. (2011). *Identity texts: The collaborative creation of power in multilingual classrooms*. Stoke on Trent, UK: Trentham Books.

Daniel, M., & Parada, K. (2008). New frontiers of literacy: Comprehension at the junction of the visual and the verbal. *International Journal of Learning, 15*(10), 18–25.

Daniel, M. C., & Huizenga-McCoy, M. (2014). Art as a medium for bilingualism and biliteracy: Suggestions from the research literature. *GIST Education and Learning Journal, 8*, 177–188.

Daniel, M.C, & Shin, D-s. (2015). Exploring New Paths to Academic Literacy for English Learners. *The Tapestry Journal, 6*(1), 1–10.

de Jong, E. J., & Harper, C. A. (2005). Preparing mainstream teachers for English language learners. Is being a good teacher good enough? *Teacher Education Quarterly, 32*(2), 102–124.

Dunn, M. W. & Finley, S. (2010). Children's struggles with the writing process: Exploring storytelling, visual arts, and keyboarding to promote narrative story writing. *Multicultural Education, 18*(1), 33–42.

Durlak, A. B., Taylor, R., Weissberg, R. P., & Schellinger, K. B. (2011). The impact of enhancing students' social and emotional learning: A meta-analysis. *Child Development, 82*(1), 405–432.

Gangwer, T. (2009). *Visual impact, visual teaching: Using images to strengthen learning*. Thousand Oaks, CA: Corwin Press.

García, O., & Wei, L. (2014). *Translanguaging: Language, bilingualism, and education*. London, England: Palgrave Macmillan.

González, N., Moll, L., and Amanti, C. (Eds.). (2005). *Funds of knowledge for teaching in Latino households*. Mahwah, NJ: Lawrence Erlbaum.

Guzetti, B. J. (2012). *Literacy in America: An encyclopedia of history, theory, and practice*. Santa Barbara, CA: ABC-CLIO Inc.

Housen, A. (2001–2002). Aesthetic thought, critical literacy and transfer. *Arts and Learning Research Journal, 18*(1), 99–132.

Housen, A., & Yenawine, P. (2016). Assessing growth. Retrieved from www.vtshome.org.

Jarvis, M. (2011). What teachers can learn from the practice of artists. *International Journal of Art & Design Education, 30*(2), 307–317.

John-Steiner, V. (1995). Cognitive pluralism: A sociocultural approach. *Mind, Culture, and Activity, 1*(2), 2–11.

Luke, A. (2003). Literacy for a new ethics of global community. *Language Arts, 81*(1), 20–22.

McNair, J. C. (2010). Classic African American children's literature. *The Reading Teacher, 64*(2), 96–105.

Rinne, L., Gregory, E., Yarmolinskaya, J., & Hardiman, M. (2011). Why arts integration improves long-term retention of content. *Mind, Brain, and Education, 5*(2), 89–96.

Rufo, D. (2011). Allowing "artistic agency" in the elementary classroom. *Art Education, 64*(3), 18–23.

Siegel, M., & Panofsky, C. P. (2009). Designs for multi-modality in literacy studies: Explorations in analysis. In K. M. Leander, R. Jimenez, M. Huntley, and V. Risko (Eds.), *58th National Reading Conference Yearbook* (pp. 99–111). Oak Creek, WI: National Reading Conference Inc.

VST. (2011). Guidelines for image selection for beginning viewers. Retrieved from www.vtshome.org.

Vygotsky, P. (2002). *Pedagogy of the oppressed*. 30th Anniversary Ed. New York: Continuum.

Yenawine, P. (1999). Theory into practice: The visual thinking strategies. Paper presented at the Aesthetic and Art Education: A Transdisciplinary Approach Conference, Calouste Gulbenkian Foundation. Lisbon, Portugal.

Yenawine, P. (2003). *Visual thinking strategies: Using art to deepen learning across school disciplines*. Cambridge, MA: Harvard Education Press.

Yenawine, P. (2005). Thoughts on visual literacy. In J. Flood, S. B. Hecht, & D. Lapp (Eds.), *Handbook of research on teaching literacy through the communicative arts* (pp. 485–846). Mahwah, NJ: Lawrence Erlbaum.

Yoon, B., Simpson, A., & Haag, C. (2010). Assimilation ideology: Critically examining underlying messages in multicultural literature. *Journal of Adolescent & Adult Literacy, 54*(2), 109–118.

Part Three

Authentic Data-Driven Evaluation

Chapter Seven

Considerations for Instruction and Assessment of ELS with Special Educational Needs

Barbara E. Marler

Implementing basic tenets of research-based pedagogy with language learners is a necessity in proper evaluation and diagnosis of students' educational needs. Culturally and linguistically responsive practices are necessary to create optimal learning environments for all learners. The author focuses the reader on how students benefit when their teachers engage in ongoing progress monitoring and offer them valid RTI interventions that provide useful formative data. She recommends a multitiered system of supports that follows an assets-based perspective.

The creation of an optimal learning environment for English learners (ELs) is our obligation as educators, whether we do so to comply with the Individuals with Disabilities Education Improvement Act of 2004 (IDEIA) or the Equal Educational Opportunities Act of 1974 (EEOA), to uphold our professional ethical standards, or to remain true to our own moral core. For ELs, most would agree that an optimal learning environment is one that incorporates the basic tenets of language-learning pedagogy and where decisions are made and carried out in efforts to increase linguistically and culturally responsive and relevant instruction, curriculum, and assessment (Marler & Sanchez-López, 2012).

Educators want to be sure that the majority of ELs are experiencing academic and linguistic success. In the rare circumstance where a language learner is struggling, we want to quickly identify the situation and intervene with appropriate interventions and progress monitoring through response to intervention (RTI) and positive behavior intervention and supports (PBIS) to redirect the student's experience toward success.

ELs come to us in the school system as either simultaneous language learners or as sequential or successive language learners. Sequential language learners were the norm in years past: children were exposed to only one language in the home and in their experiences with family, friends, and caregivers prior to school. Exposure and instruction in English commenced with their enrollment in kindergarten. Now, simultaneous language learners are the new normal (Escamilla et al., 2014). Children have been learning two languages at home, with caregivers, in preschool, and in their communities.

It is important to remember that our simultaneous language learners may show some delay in language production, and when language does appear, there may be some mixing of the languages (Hamayan & Field, 2012). Delay and mixing have no long-term negative effects and are not related in any way to observable developmental issues (Hamayan & Field, 2012). If our paradigms about language learning, our expectations about typical progress, and our understanding about appropriate instruction for ELs have not shifted to acknowledge this change, we may arrive at inaccurate conclusions when we interpret test scores and student performance data.

Oracy plays an essential role in literacy development for ELs. Ample practice in oracy activities not only builds an extensive oral language foundation, but also contributes to the development of reading skills (word recognition, grammar, and comprehension) and writing skills, for talk is practical rehearsal for writing (Escamilla et al., 2014). Oracy activities are not just beneficial for teaching survival English or limited in their influence to the beginning levels of language proficiency (Marler, 2012a). Rather, the benefit of oracy activities extends well into all content areas and all levels of language proficiency.

For many ELs, especially those in higher grades where a focus on oracy declines, there is a push to abandon oracy activities to advance to the more "rigorous" assignments in school. This practice removes a critical component of literacy instruction from many ELs' educational experience and is detrimental to their literacy development.

The National Literacy Panel on Language Minority Children and Youth (August & Shanahan, 2006) and the Center for Research on Education, Diversity, and Excellence (Genesee, Lindholm-Leary, Saunders, & Christian, 2006) published reviews of the growing body of research on literacy skill development. The following represent the main findings of those two reports and should guide our instructional planning and our interpretation and analysis of ELs' performance data (Cloud, Genesee, & Hamayan, 2009).

- Second-language literacy development is complex.
- Second- and native-language literacy development are similar in some important ways.
- Second-language literacy development differs from native-language literacy development.
- What matters depends on the learner's stage of development.

Ideally, initial literacy should be pursued in the native language. Students who are learning to read text should be able to understand it orally, otherwise they have to struggle with meaning as well as reading (Cloud, Genesee, & Hamayan, 2009). However, there are times when native initial-literacy instruction is not possible, largely when there are few speakers of the same language in an attendance center. When this situation occurs and initial literacy instruction must be offered in the student's second language, great care must be taken.

Literacy instruction should be tailored to the needs of the EL, not based on the needs of the monolingual student. Hamayan, Marler, Sanchez-López, and Damico have identified three principles about literacy development that should guide our planning and evaluation (2013).

- The most important thing about reading and writing is comprehension, not decoding letters or words or calling out words on a page.
- There is a strong connection between oral language development and learning how to read and write.
- A student's home language is a resource for developing English, not a hindrance.

Additionally, students acquire social language proficiency much sooner than they master the abstract academic English necessary to be successful in a school setting (Cummins, 2012). Margo Gottlieb defines academic language development as the course of acquiring and using different genres across the content areas and within those discourses and possessing the necessary language to process, understand, interpret, and communicate curriculum-based content (2016). Academic language development is the necessary pathway to academic achievement. As Gottlieb asserts, "to be successful in school, students must be able to process and interact in academic language as they learn content. Academic language is the glue that cements content and language learning" (2016, p. 42).

Language learners can acquire social or conversational English through exposure in and interaction with the language-majority students and teachers, but they will not learn academic language without instruction. Once again, if our paradigms for instruction in English as a second language (ESL), native–language arts, and content areas have not stretched to meet this need, ELs will struggle with content learning.

When ELs enter our school systems, they are confronted immediately with two cognitive tasks concurrently: learning a new language and learning content. Depending on the program design, ELs may receive instruction in an additive context (native–language arts instruction, content-area instruction in the native language, and ESL instruction) or they may receive instruction in a subtractive context (ESL instruction and content-area instruction in English, without native-language instruction or support).

The program design selected for implementation has a direct effect on language learning. In an additive education program, children gain English proficiency without losing proficiency in the native language or progress in academic areas. Conversely, in a subtractive education program, children gain proficiency in English at the expense of the native language and are likely to lose ground in academic subjects. The loss of the home language in the course of acquiring English can have severe social, cognitive, and academic consequences for students and their families (Hamayan, Marler, Sanchez-López, & Damico, 2013). Sometimes, the design we inherit and perpetuate or the design we implement creates a nightmare of unintended consequences for our language learners.

Our challenge is to identify, with immediacy, ELs that are struggling in school and to design and to implement plans to rectify that struggle in a manner that is sensitive to the linguistic and cultural needs of the learner. We must incorporate the basic tenets of language learning and ESL/bilingual pedagogy into our plans and into our delivery to create linguistically and culturally relevant and responsive instruction and assessment. This applies whether we are contemplating instruction provided by ESL or bilingual teachers or general education teachers, as well as how we implement response to intervention (RTI) when our ELs are experiencing difficulty in school.

Chapter 7

PRACTICAL APPLICATIONS TO THE RTI PROCESS

School-Based Teams

The first step in assembling a culturally and linguistically responsive and relevant RTI process is to create a school-based team that brings multiple professional perspectives and schemata to the table for consideration. Certainly, those with general education and special education credentials and experience must be present, but those with ESL/bilingual training and expertise are also essential.

ESL/bilingual experts on the school-based team bring their knowledge and real-world experience around language and culture to the rest of the group, contributing to the cross-pollination of professional expertise and enhancing capacity-building efforts in an attendance center. In an age of shared responsibility for all learners and the stark reality that many pre-service programs for teachers offer little to no training in English language methods and materials, increasing the understanding and skill base of all educators working with ELs is essential.

The school-based, or renamed in an assets-based perspective, solution-seeking, or declaration of possibility, team must demonstrate great facility with collegial and collaborative problem solving (Hamayan, Marler, Sanchez-López, & Damico, 2013; Block, 2008). Power and status are conferred to those that serve on any school-based team; however, teams arranged for RTI seem to be most powerful of all. Most educators would agree this is because the RTI process often serves as the entitlement and eligibility threshold for special education services (Illinois State Board of Education, 2014).

Failure to include ESL/bilingual experts on the RTI team means that pertinent questions related to the students' performance will go unasked, strengths will go unrecognized, student's performance will remain invalidated across contexts, analysis will be skewed, interventions will not be aligned to language proficiency, and progress monitoring benchmarks will be constructed in error. There is also a greater probability of disproportionality in special education placement (Hamayan, Marler, Sanchez-López, & Damico, 2013).

Additionally, this multiperspective school-based team must coach the teachers in the building to describe the student's behavior and performance before diagnosis. Many observable behaviors that ELs exhibit in school mimic those displayed by students with a disability, but there is a valid explanation for such behavior in terms of typical second-language learning.

Without ESL/bilingual experts on the team, the group will likely gravitate toward the disability explanation without any acknowledgment of the possibility of a second-language learning reason (Hamayan, Marler, Sanchez-López, & Damico, 2013). A multiperspective team needs qualitative data in descriptive form, coupled with quantitative data, to first describe with accuracy the student's performance and then to attempt to explain the student's performance with rationale from both the ESL/bilingual and the special education professional schemata.

Instruction and Intervention

In our efforts to be more culturally and linguistically relevant and responsive, we should structure both interventions and instruction to reflect the pedagogy of language learning. Interventions, like instruction for ELs, should be differentiated and scaffolded for language proficiency levels, as well as for content, processes, products, and the learning environment (Fairbairn & Jones-Vo, 2010). We do this to lessen the language load in academic learning and to render the language used for instruction more comprehensible. This is especially helpful to students who are learning subject-area content in their second language and essential for second-language proficiency to develop (Hamayan, Marler, Sanchez-López, & Damico, 2013).

Along with differentiation in the classroom, program designs and configurations for ELs should offer the means to meet ELs' needs along a continuum. We must ask how we intend to provide services to ELs with special needs, such as students with interrupted formal education (SLIFE), recently arrived immigrants and refugees, those suffering from post-traumatic stress disorder (PTSD), long-term ELs, those with gifted and talented proclivity, and those with mild to severe and profound disabilities.

Sometimes a referral for evaluation is initiated because the existing language-assistance program does not meet the needs of a particular student and the referring teacher is desperate to find help of any kind. Quite often, the path to a special education placement is well worn, not because such placement is ideal, but because it is there and known to everyone in the building (Hamayan, Marler, Sanchez-López, & Damico, 2013). Educators need to think about how they can proactively anticipate and address these special needs through the program design we establish and the range, breadth, depth, and frequency of educational services we provide.

Teachers should construct instructional activities and interventions to require active engagement in authentic use of the language. ELs need ample opportunities for rehearsal and practice, whether in oracy- or literacy-based activities. Contrived and controlled interventions, focused on discreet areas of skill or concept attainment, do not correspond with the authenticity or real-world application that best practice in language-learning pedagogy demands (Haager & Klinger, 2009).

Additionally, we should be mindful of the bridge or translanguaging aspect of learning when we plan instruction or contemplate interventions. Language learners use their knowledge of both languages and both cultures to develop literacy in both languages and to learn in academic content areas (Escamilla et al., 2014). As educators, we must first determine whether a skill or concept is universal or language specific, then we can determine whether initial instruction or intervention is necessary or if facilitation of transfer is a more appropriate strategy (Hamayan & Field, 2012).

Finally, as educators guide students into the 21st century a new orientation to accountability comes into vogue, that of shared responsibility. Gone are the days when, in terms of instruction and intervention, the responsibility was exclusively relegated to the ESL/bilingual teacher. Now, as teachers plan lessons that are tied to college and career readiness standards, which include English language development standards, the realization takes hold that progress for ELs will not be attained only through the efforts of the ESL/bilingual teachers, dedicated though they may be. Rather, the collective, collegial, and collaborative model brings together the valuable education and expertise of all professionals in the building to advance the linguistic and academic progress of ELs in their care.

Formative Assessment and Progress Monitoring

Formative assessment and progress monitoring have a close relationship. Both are intentional and systematic and have the express purpose of providing immediate feedback to adjust ongoing teaching and learning (Frey & Fisher, 2011; Gottlieb, 2016). However, in progress monitoring we often want to see a graphic display of the student's progress or response to intervention in the form of a trend line or slope of progress, and the frequency of the progress monitoring is determined by the intensity of the intervention (Illinois State Board of Education, 2014).

When addressing assessment in the context of EL, education teachers must be clear about what they are assessing and monitoring. Is the focus to be on language acquisition or on skill and concept development within a content area? The distinction between assessing academic concepts and assessing the language used to express those concepts is important for two reasons: as educators trying to address a student's struggles in school, we need to determine whether the academic performance indicates that the student did not have access to the concepts or the curriculum because of the way these were assessed or that the student's language proficiency was at too low of a level to comprehend what was presented in class (Hamayan, Marler, Sanchez-López, & Damico, 2013).

When educators are clear about what they are assessing or progress monitoring, the validity of the assessment increases (Marler, 2012b). Furthermore, they begin to explore and create assessments and progress monitoring options, such as performance-based assessments, that make the distinction between language and content crystal clear.

The basis for comparison, when judging ELs' progress and achievement, is critical. Are we establishing benchmarks based on mileposts typical of monolingual students' progress? When assessing or progress monitoring ELs, we should establish benchmarks based on their "true peers" or other similar ELs (Illinois State Board of Education, 2012). We need to guard against casting dangerously wide nets that identify students in need of reading interventions in the primary grades whose known status is language learner, not struggling reader.

A struggling reader has received instruction that has not produced competency, whereas a language learner is still in the process of acquiring language in all four domains: listening, speaking, reading, and writing. We would not expect an EL to be at grade level in reading performance in their second language while in the process of acquiring this language. Clearly, any failure to meet grade-level benchmarks calibrated to the monolingual population cannot be attributed to a reading difficulty. To gain information about typical progress in language acquisition, districts can turn to the body of research in the field of ESL/bilingual education, to the consortia that exist such as World-Class Instructional Design and Assessment (WIDA), or create their own district norms.

CONCLUSIONS AND RECOMMENDATIONS FOR ACTION

Implementation of Multitier System of Supports

While the RTI and PBIS approaches attempt to target specific areas in which students are struggling, their implementation alone will not guarantee that a school system provides an optimal learning environment that is culturally and linguistically responsive and relevant. Implementation of a multitiered system of supports (MTSS) holds more promise for that goal.

MTSS is defined as a coherent continuum of evidence-based, system-wide practices to support a rapid response to academic and behavioral needs with frequent data-based monitoring for instructional decision-making to remove barriers to learning (Castillo, Hines, Batsche, & Curtis, 2011). MTSS leverages the principles of RTI and PBIS to greater efficiency and effectiveness and activates many home, school, and community relationships to ensure student success. School systems serious about creating an optimal learning environment for students, especially ELs, should give serious consideration to adopting an MTSS approach.

Leadership from the Periphery

It is quite possible that urgency to adopt an MTSS approach may not be felt at the top of the school system's hierarchy. In this case, the existing RTI/PBIS team may need to illuminate data to create urgency and build momentum to bring about the shift. Knowledge about different leadership styles and their appropriate use in different circumstances, as well as how to lead from the middle or the periphery, is instrumental if this is the case (Robinson, 2009). Equally helpful to the team is working knowledge about different change models to utilize to describe the change in approach and to assist individuals through the change process.

Recommended Print Resources for More Information

For Every Educator

- Gottlieb, M. (2016). *Assessing English language learners: Connecting academic language proficiency to student achievement.* Thousand Oaks, CA: Corwin.
- Block, P. (2008). *Community: The structure of belonging.* San Francisco, CA: Berrett-Koehler.
- Kegan, R., & Lahey, L. (2001). *How we talk can change the way we work.* San Francisco, CA: Jossey-Bass.
- Robinson, W. (2009). *Leading people from the middle.* Bloomington, IN: Universe.

- WIDA Consortium. (2013). *RtI squared: Developing a culturally and linguistically responsive approach to response to instruction & intervention for English learners*. Madison, WI: Board of Regents of the University of Wisconsin System.
- Hamayan, E., Marler, B., Sanchez-López, C., & Damico, J. (2013). *Special education for English language learners: Delivering a continuum of services*. Philadelphia, PA: Caslon.

For General Education Teachers

- Fairbairn, S., & Jones-Vo. (2010). *Differentiating instruction and assessment for English language learners: A guide for K–12 teachers*. Philadelphia, PA: Caslon.
- de Jong, E. J. (2011). *Foundations for multilingualism in education: From principles to practice*. Philadelphia, PA: Caslon.
- Haager, D., & Klinger, J. (2009). *How to teach English language learners: Effective strategies from outstanding educators K–6*. San Francisco, CA: Jossey-Bass.

For the Reading Specialist and the Special Education Teacher

- Cloud, N., Genesee, F., & Hamayan, E. (2009). *Literacy instruction for English language learners: A teacher's guide to research-based practices*. Portsmouth, NH: Heinemann.

For the Speech-Language Therapist and the Special Education Teacher

- Paradis, J., Genesee, F., & Crago, M. (2011). *Dual language development and disorders: A handbook on bilingualism and second language learning*. Baltimore, MD: Paul H. Brookes Publishing.

For Building Administrators and Special Education Directors

- Hamayan, E., & Field, R. (2012). *English language learners at school: A guide for administrators*. Philadelphia, PA: Caslon.
- Illinois State Board of Education. (2014). *Illinois special education eligibility and entitlement procedures and criteria within a response to intervention (RTI) framework*. Retrieved from http://www.isbe.net/spec-ed/pdfs/sped_rti_framework.pdf.

Technology Applications for Use with Students

When using technology with ELs, apps and tools that are of the creation genre have much more correspondence to the basic tenets of EL pedagogy than apps and tools that attempt to replicate worksheets or provide practice on discrete, isolated skills. Apps and tools from the creation genre allow ELs to organize their knowledge or to show what they know in an authentic way. An additional consideration is to select apps that are *platform agnostic*, meaning they are not dependent on any one particular platform for functioning and are therefore accessible to students no matter what devices they may have at home.

Remind is an excellent tool for parent-school communication. It can help foster communication at home around academic learning and assist with the implementation of at-home interventions. *Padlet* allows the teacher to arrange settings to mimic a graphic organizer. It provides students with a place to collect their ideas and then reference those same ideas later in a group conversation or during a writing assignment. *Padlet* can be embedded in a website or made available through a link, so students can access the app at home and share with their parents.

Google Forms can be used in creative ways. For example, a form can be created to tap into students' daily social and emotional data if the morning activity includes answering a three-question survey on *Google Forms*. Questions such as, "How do you feel?" and "Why?" and "Do you need to talk to me?" can be included in the survey. This simple activity provides the teacher with an emotional check-in every day (even if the teacher is absent) to see what issues are impacting individual students and provide connectedness for the students with the teacher. A bonus is that *Google Forms* allows you to save responses in spreadsheet form, which may help to contextualize and explain behavior and performance over time. *Coggle* is essentially mind mapping software that can help teachers create visual supports for their instruction and can help ELs organize their learning. *PicCollage* is a photo editor that empowers students to create their own labels, to illustrate their writing, and to make their own graphic supports.

Online blogs have replaced paper dialogue journals in most classrooms. With paper dialogue journals, the amount and frequency of interaction wasn't enough, but with *online blogs*, the audience expands exponentially as does the potential feedback. Not only can students share their writing with their parents, but also with their extended families across the globe. The very likelihood of such a personal audience motivates to students to produce high quality work. For many, an *online blog* lowers anxiety because the process for editing is less cumbersome than with traditional paper.

Lastly, *YouTube* offers ELs the opportunity to practice, rehearse, and deliver oral presentations, as well as gain experience in filmmaking and editing. This technology can also help to lower the affective filter, as many prefer to perform in front of a fellow student filming instead of an in-person audience. Class-produced films are available at home so that parents can join in on the conversation about academic subject matters. Alternatively, the teacher can make a film for instruction, place it on a classroom YouTube channel, and then flip the class, asking students to view the video before instruction.

REFERENCES

August, D., & Shanahan, T. (Eds.). (2006). *Developing literacy in second language learners: Report of the national literacy panel on minority-language children and youth.* Mahwah, NJ: Lawrence Erlbaum.

Block, P. (2008). *Community: The structure of belonging.* San Francisco, CA: Berrett-Koehler.

Castillo, J. M., Hines, C. V., Batsche, G. M., & Curtis, M. J. (2011). The Florida problem solving/response to intervention project: Year 3 evaluation report. Retrieved from: http://www.floridarti.usf.edu/resources/format/pdf/yr3_eval_report.pdf.

Cloud, N., Genesee, F., & Hamayan, E. (2009). *Literacy instruction for English language learners: A teacher's guide to research-based practices.* Portsmouth, NH: Heinemann.

Cummins, J. (2012). How long does it take for an English language learner to become proficient in a second language? In E. Hamayan & R. Freeman Fields (Eds.), *English language learners at school: A guide for administrators* (2nd ed., pp. 37–39). Philadelphia, PA: Caslon.

de Jong, E. J. (2011). *Foundations for multilingualism in education: From principles to practice.* Philadelphia, PA: Caslon.

Equal Educational Opportunities Act of 1974 (EEOA), 20 U.S.C. § 1703(f) (Supp. 1984).

Escamilla, K., Hopewell, S., Butvilofsky, S., Sparrow, W., Soltero-González, L., Ruiz-Figueroa, O., & Escamilla, M. (2014). *Biliteracy from the start: Literacy squared in action.* Philadelphia, PA: Caslon.

Fairbairn, S., & Jones-Vo, S. (2010). *Differentiating instruction and assessment for English language learners: A guide for K–12 teachers.* Philadelphia, PA: Caslon.

Frey, N., & Fisher, D. (2011). *The formative action assessment plan: Practical steps to more successful teaching and learning.* Alexandria, VA: ASCD.

Genesee, F., Lindholm-Leary, K., Saunders, W., & Christian, D. (2006). *Educating English language learners: A synthesis of empirical evidence.* New York: Cambridge University Press.

Gottlieb, M. (2016). *Assessing English language learners: Connecting academic language proficiency to student achievement.* Thousand Oaks, CA: Corwin.

Haager, D., & Klinger, J. (2009). *How to teach English language learners: Effective strategies from outstanding educators K–6.* San Francisco, CA: Jossey-Bass.

Hamayan, E., & Field, R. (2012). *English language learners at school: A guide for administrators*. Philadelphia, PA: Caslon.

Hamayan, E., Marler, B., Sanchez-López, C., & Damico, J. (2013). *Special education for English language learners: Delivering a continuum of services*. Philadelphia, PA: Caslon.

Illinois State Board of Education. (2014). *Illinois special education eligibility and entitlement procedures and criteria within a response to intervention (RTI) framework*. Retrieved from http://www.isbe.net/spec-ed/pdfs/sped_rti_framework.pdf.

Individuals with Disabilities Education Improvement Act, 20 U.S.C. § 1400 (2004).

Kegan, R., & Lahey, L. (2001). *How we talk can change the way we work*. San Francisco, CA: Jossey-Bass.

Marler, B. (2012a). How can we best serve students who come with interrupted formal education (SIFE) or limited prior schooling? In E. Hamayan & R. Freeman Fields (Eds.), *English language learners at school: A guide for administrators* (2nd ed., pp. 213–214). Philadelphia, PA: Caslon.

Marler, B. (2012b). How can we provide valid and reliable evidence of English language learner student growth and how can we use that evidence for decision-making? In E. Hamayan & R. Freeman Fields (Eds.), *English language learners at school: A guide for administrators* (2nd ed., pp. 85–87). Philadelphia, PA: Caslon.

Marler, B., & Sanchez-López, C. (2012). How can we ensure that response to intervention (RTI) is appropriate for English language learners? In E. Hamayan & R. Freeman Fields (Eds.), *English language learners at school: A guide for administrators* (2nd ed., pp. 207–208). Philadelphia, PA: Caslon.

Paradis, J., Genesee, F., & Crago, M. (2011). *Dual language development and disorders: A handbook on bilingualism and second language learning*. Baltimore, MD: Paul H. Brookes Publishing.

Robinson, W. (2009). *Leading people from the middle*. Bloomington, IN: Universe.

WIDA Consortium. (2013). *RtI squared: Developing a culturally and linguistically responsive approach to response to instruction & intervention for English learners*. Madison, WI: Board of Regents of the University of Wisconsin System.

References

Abu El-Haj, T. R. (2006). *Elusive justice: Wrestling with difference and educational equity in everyday practice*. New York: Routledge.

Allen, K. (2016). *Restorying literacy: The role of anomaly in shifting perceptions of college readers*. (Doctoral dissertation). Available from ProQuest Dissertations & Theses Global.

Allen, K., & Goodman, K. (In press). Revaluing reading. In J. Damico & M. Ball (Eds.), *Sage encyclopedia of human communication sciences and disorders*. Thousand Oaks, CA: Sage Publications.

Arnheim, R. (2004). *Visual thinking*. (Paperback Edition). Berkeley, CA: University of California Press.

Au, K., Carroll, J., & Scheu, J. (2001). *Balanced literacy instruction: A teacher resource book*. Norwood, MA: Christopher-Gordon Publishers, Inc.

August, D., & Shanahan, T. (Eds.). (2006). *Developing literacy in second-language learners. A report of the National Literacy Panel on Language-Minority Children and Youth*. Mahwah, NJ: Lawrence Erlbaum.

Bafna, S. (2016). Personal interview.

Baker, C. (2011). *Foundations of bilingual education and bilingualism* (5th ed.). Clevedon, UK: Multilingual Matters.

Beck, I. L., McKeown, M. G., & Kucan, L. (2013). *Bringing words to life: Robust vocabulary instruction*, 2nd ed. New York: Guilford Press.

Beeman, K., & Urow, C. (2013). Teaching for biliteracy: Strengthening bridges between languages. Philadelphia, PA: Caslon Publishing.

Beninghof, A., & Leensvaart, M. (2016). Co-teaching to support ELLs. *Educational Leadership*, 70–74.

Berg, H., Petrón, M., & Greybeck, B. (2012). Setting the foundation for working with English language learners in the secondary classroom. *American Secondary Education, 40*(3), 34–44.

Bernhard, J. K., Cummins, J., Campoy, F. A., Ada, A. F., Winsler, A., & Bleiker, C. (2006). Identity texts and literacy development among preschool English language learners: Enhancing learning opportunities for children at risk of learning disabilities. *Teachers College Record, 108*, 2380–2405.

Bialystok, E. (2011). Reshaping the mind: The benefits of bilingualism. *Canadian Journal of Experimental Psychology, 65*(4), 229–235.

Bialystok, E., Luk, G., & Kwan, E. (2005). Bilingualism, biliteracy, and learning to read: Interactions among languages and writing systems. *Scientific Studies of Reading, 9*(1), 43–61.

Bishop, R. S. (1990). Mirrors, windows, and sliding glass doors. *Perspectives: Choosing and Using Books for the Classroom, 6*(3), ix–xi.

Block, P. (2008). *Community: The structure of belonging.* San Francisco, CA: Berrett-Koehler.

Bridgeland, J., Bruce, M., & Hariharan, A. (2013). The missing piece: A national teacher survey of how emotional and social learning can empower children and transform schools. Civic Enterprises and Peter D. Hart Research Associates. *Collaborative for Academic, Social, and Emotional Learning*, 1–60.

Brisk, M. E. (2006). *Bilingual Education: From Compensatory to Quality Education.* Mahwah, NJ: Lawrence Erlbaum.

Brisk, M. E. (2008). *Language, culture, and community in teacher education.* Mahwah, NJ: Lawrence Erlbaum (for the American Association of Colleges for Teacher Education).

Brisk, M. E. (2015). *Engaging students in academic literacies: Genre-based pedagogy for K–5 classrooms.* New York: Routledge.

Brisk, M. E., Burgos, A., & Hamerla, S. (2004). *Situational context of education: A window into the world of bilingual learners.* Mahwah, NJ: Lawrence Erlbaum.

Brisk, M. E., & Harrington, M. M. (2000). *Literacy and bilingualism: A handbook for all teachers.* Mahwah, NJ: Lawrence Erlbaum.

Brisk, M. E., & Proctor, C. P. (2012). *Challenges and supports for English language learners in bilingual programs.* Paper Presented at the Understanding Language Conference. Palo Alto, CA: Stanford University.

Brisk, M. E., & Proctor, C. P. (2015). What do the Common Core State Standards mean for bilingual education? In G. Valdés, K. Menken, & M. Castro (Eds.), *Common core bilingual and English language learners* (pp. 15–16). Philadelphia, PA: Caslon Publishing.

Brooks, K., Adams, S. R., & Morita-Mullaney, T. (2010). Creating inclusive learning communities for students: Transforming school principals' perspectives. *Theory into Practice, 49*, 145–151.

Brown, S., & Larson-Hall, J. (2012). *Second language acquisition myths: Applying second language research to classroom teaching.* Ann Arbor, Michigan: University of Michigan Press.

Brummet, B., & Maras, L. (1995). Liberated by miscues: Students and teachers discovering the reading process. *Primary Voices, 3*(4), 23–31.

Calderon, M., Slavin, R., & Sanchez, M. (2011). Effective instruction for English learners. *The Future of Children, 21*(1), 103–127.

Cambourne, B. (1995). Towards an educationally relevant theory of literacy learning: Twenty years of inquiry. *The Reading Teacher, 49*(3), 182–192.

Canagarajah, A. S. (2011). Translanguaging in the classroom: Emerging issues for research and pedagogy. *Applied Linguistics Review, 2*, 1–28.

Canagarajah, A. S. (Ed.). (2013). *Literacy as translingual practice: Between communities and classrooms.* New York: Routledge.

Canagarajah, S. (2013). *Translingual practice: Global Englishes and cosmopolitan relations.* Abingdon, UK: Routledge.

Carrasquillo, A., & Rodriguez, J. (1998). Measuring success in bilingual education programs: Case studies of exemplary practices. *Reports-Evaluative*, 2–14.

Carrejo, D., Cortez, T., & Reinhartz, J. (2010). Exploring principal leadership roles within a community of practice to promote science performance of English Language Learners. *Academic Leadership, 8*(4).
Carroll, P. E., & Bailey, A. L. (2016). Do decision rules matter? A descriptive study of English language proficiency assessment classifications for English-language learners and native English speakers in fifth grade. *Language Testing, 33*(1), 23–52. doi:10.1177/0265532215576380.
Carter, T. P., & Chatfield, M. L. (1986). Effective bilingual schools: Implications for policy and practice. *American Journal of Education, 95* (l), 200–232.
Castañeda, M., Rodríguez-González, E., & Schulz, M. (2011). Enhancing reading proficiency in English language learners (ELLs): The importance of knowing your ELL in mainstream classrooms. *Tapestry Journal, 3*(1), 38–63.
Castillo, J. M., Hines, C. V., Batsche, G. M., & Curtis, M. J. (2011). The Florida problem solving/response to intervention project: Year 3 evaluation report. Retrieved from: http://www.floridarti.usf.edu/resources/format/pdf/yr3_eval_report.pdf.
Cazden, C. B. (1984). Effective instructional practices in bilingual education. [Research review commissioned by the National Institute of Education] (ERIC Document Reproduction Service No. ED 249 768).
Celic C., & Seltzer, K. (2011). Translanguaging: A CUNY-NYSIEB guide for educators. Retrieved May 25, 2016, at http://www.nysieb.ws.gc.cuny.edu/files/2012/06/FINAL-Translanguaging-Guide-With-Cover-1.pdf.
Cenoz, J., & Gorter, D. (2011). Focus on multilingualism: A study of trilingual writing. *The Modern Language Journal, 95*(3), 356–369.
Chang, C. (2016). Personal communication, October 3.
Choi, D. S., & Morrison, P. (2014). Learning to get it right: Understanding change processes in professional development for teachers of English learners. *Professional Development in Education, 40*(3), 416–435.
Cloud, N., Genesee, F., & Hamayan, E. (2009). *Literacy instruction for English language learners: A teacher's guide to research-based practices*. Portsmouth, NH: Heinemann.
Coady, M., Hamann, E. T., Harrington, M., Pacheco, M., Pho, S., & Yedlin, J. (2008). Successful schooling for ELLs: Principles for building responsive learning environments. In L. S. Verplaetse & N. Migliacci (Eds.), *Inclusive pedagogy for English language learners: A handbook of research-informed practices* (pp. 245–255). New York: Lawrence Erlbaum.
Coleman, R., & Goldenberg, C. (2010). What does research say about effective practices for English learners? Part IV: Models for schools and districts. *Kappa Delta Pi Record, 46*(4), 156–163.
Collier, V. P., & Thomas, W. P. (2014). *Creating dual language schools for a transformed world: Administrators' speak*. Albuquerque, NM: Fuentes Press.
Committee for Children. (2016). How social-emotional learning helps children succeed in schools, the workplace, and life. Retrieved from www.cfchildren.org.
Common Core State Standards. (2010). Common Core State Standards for English Language Arts & Literacy in History / Social Studies, Science, and Technical Subjects. Retrieved from www.corestandards.org.
Craighead, E., & Ramanathan, H. (2007). Effective teacher interactions with English language learners in mainstream classes. *Research in the Schools, 14*(1), 60–71.
Creese, A., & Blackledge, A. (2010). Translanguaging in the bilingual classroom: A pedagogy for learning and teaching? *Modern Language Journal, 94*(1), 103–115.
Crowell, C. (1995). Documenting the strengths of bilingual readers. *Primary Voices, 3*(4), 32–38. Retrieved from http://www.ncte.org/journals/pv/issues/v3-4.

Crowell, C. (2015). Miscue analysis V. DIBELS: A tale of resistance. *Talking Points*, *26*(2), 2–9.

Cummins, J. (1979). Linguistic interdependence and the educational development of bilingual children. *Review of Educational Research, 49*, 222–251.

Cummins, J. (2005). Teaching for cross-language transfer in dual language education: Possibilities and pitfalls. *TESOL Symposium on Dual Language Education: Teaching and Learning Two Languages in the EFL Setting*. September 23, 2005, Boğaziçi University, Istanbul, Turkey.

Cummins, J. (2009). Pedagogies of choice: Challenging coercive relations of power in classrooms and communities. *International Journal of Bilingual Education and Bilingualism*, *2*(3), 261–271.

Cummins, J. (2012). How long does it take for an English language learner to become proficient in a second language? In E. Hamayan & R. Freeman Fields (Eds.), *English language learners at school: A guide for administrators* (2nd ed., pp. 37–39). Philadelphia, PA: Caslon Publishing.

Cummins, J., Bismilla, V., Chow, P., Cohen, S., Giampapa, F., Leoni, L., Sandhu, P., & Sastri, P. (2005). Affirming identity in multilingual classrooms. *Educational Leadership*, *63*(1), 38–43.

Cummins, J., & Early, M. (2011). *Identity texts: The collaborative creation of power in multilingual classrooms*. Stoke-on-Trent, UK: Trentham Books.

Cunningham, P. M., & Allington, R. L. (2007). *Classroom that work: They can all read and write*, 4th ed. Boston, MA: Pearson Education.

Curtin, E. M. (2005). Teaching Practices for ESL Students. *Multicultural Education*, *12*(3), 22–27.

Daniel, M. (2016). Critical pedagogy's power in English language teaching. In L. R. Jacobs & C. Hastings (Eds.), *The importance of social justice in English language teaching* (pp. 25–38). Alexandria, VA: TESOL Press.

Daniel, M., & Parada, K. (2008). New frontiers of literacy: Comprehension at the junction of the visual and the verbal. *International Journal of Learning*, *15*(10), 18–25.

Daniel, M. C. (2010). La preparación del maestro: Una examinación de las voces de los capacitadores que enseñan en las escuelas normales de Guatemala. *Education and Learning Research Journal, GIST*, *4*(1), 127–137.

Daniel, M. C., & Huizenga-McCoy, M. (2014). Art as a medium for bilingualism and biliteracy: Suggestions from the research literature. *GIST Education and Learning Journal*, *8*, 177–188.

Daniel, M. C., & Shin, D-S. (2015). Exploring new paths to academic literacy for English learners. *The Tapestry Journal, (6)*1, 1–10.

Davenport, M. (2002). *Miscues not mistakes: Reading assessment in the classroom*. Portsmouth, NH: Heinemann.

Davis, V. (2014). A guidebook for social media in the classroom. Retrieved February 11, 2016, from http://www.edutopia.org/blog/guidebook-social-media-in-classroom- vicki-davis.

de Jong, E. (2013). Preparing mainstream teachers for multilingual classrooms. *Association of Mexican-American Educators*, *7*(2), 40–50.

de Jong, E. J. (2006). Integrated bilingual education: An alternative approach. *Bilingual Research Journal*, *30*(1), 23–44.

de Jong, E. J. (2011a). A review of "Towards multilingual education: Basque educational research from an international perspective." *Language & Education: An International Journal, 25*(1), 82–84. doi:10.1080/09500782.2010.494859.

de Jong, E. J. (2011b). *Foundations for multilingualism in education: From principles to practice.* Philadelphia, PA: Caslon Publishing.
de Jong, E. J., & Derrick-Mescua, M. (2003). Refining preservice teachers' questions for second language learners: Higher order thinking for all levels of language proficiency. *Sunshine State TESOL Journal, 2*(2), 29–37.
de Jong, E. J., & Freeman, R. (2010). Bilingual approaches. In Leung, C., and Creese, A. (Eds.) *English as an Additional Language: Approaches to Teaching Linguistic Minority Students.* (pp. 108–122). London: Sage.
de Jong, E. J., Gort, M., & Cobb, C. D. (2005). Bilingual education within the context of English-only policies: Three districts' responses to Question 2 in Massachusetts. *Educational Policy, 19*(4), 595–620.
de Jong, E. J., & Harper, C. A. (2005). Preparing mainstream teachers for English-language learners: Is being a good teacher good enough? *Teacher Education Quarterly, 32*(2), 101–124.
de Jong, E. J., & Lopez Estrada, P. (2011). The role of a teacher in structuring peer interaction. *Sunshine State TESOL Journal, 10* (1), 1–7.
de Oliveira, L. C., Gilmetdinova, A., & Pelaez Morales, C. (2015). The use of Spanish by a monolingual kindergarten teacher to support English language learners. *Language and Education, 29*(6), 1–21.
Deussen, T., Autio, E., Miller, B., Lockwood, A. T., & Stewart, V. (2008). *What teachers should know about instruction for English language learners: A report to Washington State.* Portland: NWREL.
Dickinson, D. K., McCabe, A., Clark-Chiarelli, N., & Wolf, A. (2004). Cross-language transfer of phonological awareness in low-income Spanish and English bilingual preschool children. *Applied Psycholinguistics, 25*(3), 323–347. doi: 10.1017/S0142716404001158.
Dunn, M. W., & Finley, S. (2010). Children's struggles with the writing process: Exploring storytelling, visual arts, and keyboarding to promote narrative story writing. *Multicultural Education, 18*(1), 33–42.
Durlak, A. B., Taylor, R., Weissberg, R. P., & Schellinger, K. B. (2011). The impact of enhancing students' social and emotional learning: A meta-analysis. *Child Development, 82*(1), 405–432.
Dworin, J. E. (April 1, 2003). Insights into biliteracy development: Toward a bidirectional theory of bilingual pedagogy. *Journal of Hispanic Higher Education, 2*(2), 171–186.
Echevarria, J., Vogt, M. E., & Short, D. (2014). *Making content comprehensible for elementary English learners: The SIOP® model.* Second Edition. Boston: Allyn & Bacon.
Edelsky, C. (1991). *With literacy and justice for all: Rethinking the social in language and education.* London: Falmer Press.
Edelsky, C. K. (1986). *Writing in a bilingual program. Había una vez.* Norwood, NJ: Ablex Publishing.
Elfers, A. M., & Stritikus, T. (2013). How school and district leaders support classroom teachers' work with English language learners. *Educational Administration Quarterly, 20*(10), 1–40.
Equal Educational Opportunities Act of 1974 (EEOA), 20 U.S.C. § 1703(f) (Supp. 1984).
Ernst-Slavit, G., & Mulhern, M. (2003). Bilingual books: Promoting literacy and biliteracy in the second-language and mainstream classroom. *Reading Online,* 1–13.
Escamilla, K., Hopewell, S., Butvilofsky, S., Sparrow, W., Soltero-González, L., Ruiz-Figueroa, O., & Escamilla, M. (2014). *Biliteracy from the start: Literacy squared in action.* Philadelphia, PA: Caslon Publishing.

Evans, B. A., & Hornberger, N. H. (2005). No child left behind: Repealing and "unpeeling" federal language education policy in the United States. *Language Policy, 4* (1), 87–106. http://dx.doi.org/10.1007/s10993-004-6566-2.

Ewald, J. (2005). Language-related episodes in an assessment context: A "small-group quiz." *The Canadian Modern Language Review, 61*(4), 565–586.

Fairbairn, S., & Jones-Vo, S. (2010). *Differentiating instruction and assessment for English language learners: A guide for K–12 teachers.* Philadelphia, PA: Caslon Publishing.

Ferreiro, E., & Teberosky, A. (1982). *Literacy before schooling.* Exeter, NH: Heinemann Educational Books.

Fishman, J. (1980). Ethnocultural dimensions in the acquisition and retention of biliteracy. *Journal of Basic Writing, 3*, 48–61.

Freeman, A. (2001). The eyes have it: Oral miscue and eye movement analysis of the reading of fourth grade Spanish/English bilinguals. (Doctoral dissertation). Available from ProQuest Dissertations & Theses Global.

Freeman, Y., Freeman, D., & Mercuri, S. (2003). Helping middle and high school age English language learners achieve academic success. *NABE Journal of Research and Practice*, Winter, 110–122.

Frey, N., & Fisher, D. (2011). *The formative action assessment plan: Practical steps to more successful teaching and learning.* Alexandria, VA: ASCD.

Funds of Knowledge – A look at Luis Moll's research into hidden family resources. (n.d.). Retrieved May 1, 2016, from https://edsource.org/wp-content/uploads/old/Luis_Moll_Hidden_Family_Resources.pdf.

Galguera, T., & Hakuta, K. (1997). Linguistically diverse students. In H. J. Walberg & G. D. Haertel (Eds.), *Psychology and Educational Practice* (pp. 387–407). Berkeley, CA: McCutchan Publishers.

Gándara, P., & Hopkins, M. (Eds.). (2010). *Forbidden language: English learners and restrictive language policies.* New York: Teachers College Press.

Gangwer, T. (2009). *Visual impact, visual teaching: Using images to strengthen learning.* Thousand Oaks, CA: Corwin Press.

Garbati, J. F., & Mady, C. J. (2015). Oral Skill Development in Second Languages: A Review in Search of Best Practices. *Theory & Practice in Language Studies, 5*(9), 1663–1770. doi:10.17507/tpls.0509.01.

García, C., & Chun, H. (2016). Culturally responsive teaching and teacher expectations for Latino middle school students. *Journal of Latina/o Psychology.* doi:10.1037/lat0000061.

García, O. (2008). Teaching Spanish and Spanish in teaching in the U.S.: Integrating bilingual perspectives. In C. Helot & A. M. de Mejía (Eds.), *Forging multilingual spaces: Integrating majority and minority bilingual education* (pp. 31–57). Clevedon, United Kingdom: Multilingual Matters.

García, O. (2009). *Bilingual education in the 21st century: A global perspective.* Malden, MA: Wiley-Blackwell.

García, O. (2015). How should we refer to students who are acquiring English as an additional language? In G. Valdés, K. Menken, & M. Castro (Eds.), *Common core bilingual and English language learners* (pp. 23–24). Philadelphia, PA: Caslon Publishing.

García, O., & Flores, N. (2013). Multilingualism and Common Core State Standards in the U.S. In S. May (Ed.). *The multilingual turn: Implications for SLA, TESOL, and bilingual education.* New York: Routledge.

García, O., & Wei, L. (2014). *Translanguaging: Language, bilingualism, and education.* London, England: Palgrave Macmillan.

García, O., & Yip, J. (2015). Introduction: Translanguaging: Practice briefs for educators. *Theory, Research and Action in Urban Education, 4*(1).

Genesee, F., Lindholm-Leary, K., Saunders, W., & Christian, D. (2006). *Educating English language learners: A synthesis of empirical evidence.* New York: Cambridge University Press.

Gersten, R., & Baker, S. (2000). Practices for English language learners. *Special Education Programs*, 1–12.

Gersten, R., Baker, S. K., Shanahan, T., Linan-Thompson, S., Collins, P., & Scarcella, R. (2007). *Effective literacy and English language instruction for English learners in the elementary grades: A practice guide* (NCEE 2007-4011). Washington, DC: National Center for Education Evaluation and Regional Assistance, Institute of Education Sciences, U.S. Department of Education. Retrieved from http://ies.ed.gov/ncee.

Giambo, D., & Szecsi, T. (2015). Promoting and maintaining bilingualism and biliteracy: Cognitive and biliteracy benefits & strategies for monolingual teachers. *The Open Communication Journal*, 56–60.

Glogster EDU. (2016). Boston, MA: Glogster EC Inc.

Gold, N. (2006). *Successful bilingual schools: Six effective programs in California.* San Diego: San Diego County Office of Education.

Goldenberg, C. (2008). Teaching English language learners: What the research does—and does not—say. *American Educator*, 8–44.

González, N. (2015, December). Imagining literacy equity: *Theorizing flows of community practices.* Plenary Address presented at Literacy Research Association, Carlsbad, CA.

González, N., Moll, L., & Amanti, C. (Eds.). (2005). *Funds of knowledge for teaching in Latino households.* Mahwah, NJ: Lawrence Erlbaum.

Goodman, K. (1976). Miscues: Windows on the reading process. In K. Goodman (Ed.), *Miscue analysis: Applications to reading instruction* (pp. 3–14). Urbana, IL: ERIC Clearing House.

Goodman, K., Fries, P., & Strauss, S. (2016). *Reading the grand illusion: How and why people make sense of print.* New York: Routledge.

Goodman, K., & Goodman, Y. (2014). *Making sense of learners making sense of written language: The selected works of Kenneth S. Goodman & Yetta M. Goodman.* New York: Routledge.

Goodman, K., Goodman, Y., & Allen, K. (2016). Research on helping readers make sense of print: Evolution of comprehension based pedagogy. In S. Israel (Ed.), *Handbook of research on reading comprehension* (Vol. II). New York: Guilford Press.

Goodman, K., Goodman, Y., & Flores, B. (1979). *Reading in the bilingual classroom: Literacy and biliteracy.* Rosslyn, VA: Interamerica.

Goodman, K., Wang, S., Iventosch, M., & Goodman, Y. (2011). *Reading in Asian languages: Making sense of written texts in Chinese, Japanese and Korean.* New York: Routledge.

Goodman, Y. (1990). *How children construct literacy: Piagetian perspectives.* Newark, DE: International Reading Association.

Goodman, Y. (1996a). Kidwatching: An alternative to testing. In S. Wilde (Ed.), *Notes from a kidwatcher: Selected writings of Yetta M. Goodman* (pp. 211–218). Portsmouth, NH: Heinemann.

Goodman, Y. (1996b). Revaluing readers while readers revalue themselves: Retrospective Miscue Analysis. *Reading Teacher, 49*(8), 600–609.

Goodman, Y., & Anders, P. (1999). Listening to Erica read: Perceptions and analyses from six perspectives. In T. Shanahan, F. Rodriguez-Brown, C. Worthman, et al. (Eds.), *The forty-eighth yearbook of National Reading Conference* (pp. 178–198). Chicago, IL: National Reading Conference, Inc.

Goodman, Y., & Flurkey, A. (1996). Retrospective miscue analysis in middle school. In Y. Goodman & A. Marek (Eds.), *Retrospective miscue analysis: Revaluing readers and reading* (pp. 87–105). Katonah, NY: Richard C. Owen Publishers.

Goodman, Y., Martens, A., & Flurkey, P. (2014). *Retrospective miscue analysis: A window into readers' thinking*. Katonah, NY: Richard C. Owen Publishers.

Goodman, Y., Martens, A., & Flurkey, P. (2016). Revaluing readers: Learning from Zachary. *Language Arts, 93*(3), 213–225.

Goodman, Y. M. (2003). *Valuing language study: Inquiry into language for elementary and middle schools*. Urbana, IL: National Council of Teachers of English.

Goodman, Y. M., Watson, D. J., & Burke, C. L. (2005). *Reading miscue inventory: from evaluation to instruction*. Katonah, NY: Richard C. Owen Publishers.

Gorski, P. C. (2013). *Reaching and teaching students in poverty*. New York: Teachers College Press.

Gort, M., de Jong, E. J., & Cobb, C. D. (2008). Seeing through a bilingual lens: Structural and ideological contexts of sheltered English immersion in three Massachusetts districts. *Journal of Educational Research and Policy Studies, 8*(2), 41–66.

Gottlieb, M. (2016). *Assessing English language learners: Connecting academic language proficiency to student achievement*. Thousand Oaks, CA: Corwin Press.

Gregory, E. (2008). *Learning to read in a new language: Making sense of words and worlds*. Thousand Oaks, CA: Sage Publications.

Grosjean, F. (2008). *Studying bilinguals*. New York: Oxford University Press.

Guzetti, B. J. (2012). *Literacy in America: An encyclopedia of history, theory, and practice*. Santa Barbara, CA: ABC-CLIO Inc.

Haager, D., & Klinger, J. (2009). *How to teach English language learners: Effective strategies from outstanding educators K–6*. San Francisco, CA: Jossey-Bass.

Halliday, M. (2003). Three aspects of children's language development: Learning language, learning through language, learning about language (1980). In J. Webster (Ed.), *The language of early childhood, Volume 4: The collected works of M.A.K. Halliday* (pp. 308–326). London: Continuum.

Hamayan, E., & Field, R. (2012). *English language learners at school: A guide for administrators*. Philadelphia, PA: Caslon Publishing.

Hamayan, E., Marler, B., Sanchez-López, C., & Damico, J. (2013). *Special education for English language learners: Delivering a continuum of services*. Philadelphia, PA: Caslon Publishing.

Han, Y. C. (2012). From survivors to leaders: Stages of immigrant parents involvement. In E. G. Kugler (Ed.), *Innovative voices in education: Engaging diverse communities* (pp. 171–186). Lanham, MD: Rowman & Littlefield.

Haneda, M., & Wells, G. (2012). Some key pedagogic principles for helping ELLs to succeed in school. *Theory into Practice, 51*, 297–304.

Herrell, A., & Jordan, M. (2011). *Fifty strategies for teaching English language learners*, 4th ed. Upper Saddle River, NJ: Pearson Education.

Hesson, S., Seltzer, K., & Woodley. H. H. (2014). *Translanguaging in curriculum & instruction: A CUNY-NYSEIB guide for educators*. New York: CUNY-NYSEIB.

Hill, J., & Flynn, K. (2008). Asking the right question. *National Staff Development Council, 29*(1), 46–52.

Honigsfeld, A., & Dove, M. G. (2010). *Collaboration and co-teaching. Strategies for English learners*. Thousand Oaks, CA: Corwin Press.

Hopewell, S., & Escamilla, K. (2014). Biliteracy development in immersion contexts. *Journal of Immersion and Content-based Language Education, 2*(2), 181–195.

Hornberger, N. H. (2002). Multilingual language policies and the continua of biliteracy: An ecological approach. *Language Policy, 1*(1), 27–51.
Hornberger, N. H., & Ricento, T. (1996). Language planning and policy and the ELT profession. *Special topic issue, TESOL Quarterly, 30*(3), 401–427.
Horwitz, A. R., Uro, G., Price-Baugh, R., Simon, C., Uzzell, R., Lewis, S., & Casserly, M. (2009). *Succeeding with English language learners: Lessons learned from the great city schools*. The Council of the Great City Schools.
Housen, A. (2001–2002). Aesthetic thought, critical literacy and transfer. *Arts and Learning Research Journal, 18*(1), 99–132.
Housen, A., & Yenawine, P. (2016). Assessing growth. Retrieved from www.vtshome.org.
Hudelson, S. (1987). The role of native language literacy in the education of language minority children. *Language Arts, 64*(8), 827–841.
Illinois State Board of Education. (2014). *Illinois special education eligibility and entitlement procedures and criteria within a response to intervention (RTI) framework*. Retrieved from http://www.isbe.net/spec-ed/pdfs/sped_rti_framework.pdf.
Individuals with Disabilities Education Improvement Act, 20 U.S.C. § 1400 (2004).
Islam, C., & Park, M. (2015). Preparing teachers to promote culturally relevant teaching: Helping English language learners in the classroom. *Multicultural Education*, 39–43.
Jarvis, M. (2011). What teachers can learn from the practice of artists. *International Journal of Art & Design Education, 30*(2), 307–317.
John-Steiner, V. (1995). Cognitive pluralism: A sociocultural approach. *Mind, Culture, and Activity, 1*(2), 2–11.
Kegan, R., & Lahey, L. (2001). *How we talk can change the way we work*. San Francisco, CA: Jossey-Bass.
Kim, M. (2010). *Adult ESL Korean readers' responses about their reading in L1 Korean and L2 English*. (Doctoral dissertation). Available from ProQuest Dissertations and Theses database (UMI No. 3402930).
Kopriva, R. J., Emick, J. E., Hipolito-Delgado, C. P., & Cameron, C. A. (2007). Do proper accommodation assignments make a difference? Examining the impact of improved decision making on scores for English language learners. *Educational Measurement: Issues & Practice, 26*(3), 11–20. doi:10.1111/j.1745-3992.2007.00097.x.
Kramsch, C. (2014). Teaching foreign languages in an era of globalization: An introduction. *The Modern Language Journal, 98*(1), 296–311.
Krumgold, J., & Charlot, J. (1953). *And now Miguel*. New York: Thomas Y. Crowell.
Kumashiro, K. (2004). *Against common sense: Teaching and learning toward social justice*. New York: Routledge Falmer.
Langer, J. A., Bartolomé, L., Vasquez, O., & Lucas, T. (1990). Meaning construction in school literacy tasks: A study of bilingual students. *American Educational Research Journal, 27*, 427–471.
Lesaux, N. K., & Harris, J. R. (2015). *Cultivating knowledge, building language: Literacy instruction for English learners in elementary school*. Portsmouth, NH: Heinemann.
Li, J. (2012). Principles of effective English language learners' pedagogy. *Research in Review, 3*, 1–20.
Liwanag, M. P. S. U. (2006). *Affect in secondary students' reading as revealed by their emotional responses in retrospective miscue analysis*. (Doctoral dissertation). Available from ProQuest Dissertations & Theses Global. (305353120).
Lohse, K. (1998). Writing letters: Moving from invention to convention in a bilingual kindergarten. Unpublished Teacher Research Project, University of Arizona.

López, F., & Iribarren, J. (2014). Creating and sustaining inclusive instructional settings for English language learners: Why, what, and how. *Theory into Practice, 53*, 106–114.

Lucas, T., & Villegas, A. M. (2013). Preparing linguistically responsive teachers: Laying the foundation in preservice teacher education, *Theory into Practice, 52*(2), 98–109.

Lucero, A. (2014). Teachers' use of linguistic scaffolding to support the academic language development of first-grade emergent bilingual students. *Journal of Early Childhood Literacy, 14*(4), 534–561. doi:10.1177/1468798413512848.

Luke, A. (2003). Literacy for a new ethics of global community. *Language Arts, 81*(1), 20–22.

Lyster, R. (2004). Differential effects of prompts and recasts in form-focused instruction. *Studies in Second Language Acquisition, 26*, 399–432.

Mace-Matluck, B. J. (1982, June). Literacy instruction in bilingual settings: A synthesis of current research. (Professional Papers M-1. Los Alamitos, CA: National Center for Bilingual Research) (ERIC Document Reproduction Service No. ED 222 079).

Mace-Matluck, B. J. (1990). The effective schools movement: Implications for Title VII and Bilingual Education Projects. *Annual Conference Journal NABE '88–89* (pp. 83–95). Washington, DC: NABE.

Mancilla-Martínez, J., Pan, B. A., & Vagh, S. V. (2011). Assessing the productive vocabulary of Spanish-English bilingual toddlers from low-income families. *Applied Psycholinguistics, 32*, 333–357. doi:10.1017/S0142716410000433.

Marler, B. (2012a). How can we best serve students who come with interrupted formal education (SIFE) or limited prior schooling? In E. Hamayan & R. Freeman Fields (Eds.), *English language learners at school: A guide for administrators* (2nd ed., pp. 213–214). Philadelphia, PA: Caslon Publishing.

Marler, B. (2012b). How can we provide valid and reliable evidence of English language learner student growth and how can we use that evidence for decision-making? In E. Hamayan & R. Freeman Fields (Eds.), *English language learners at school: A guide for administrators* (2nd ed., pp. 85–87). Philadelphia, PA: Caslon Publishing.

Marler, B. & Sanchez-López, C. (2012). How can we ensure that response to intervention (RTI) is appropriate for English language learners? In E. Hamayan & R. Freeman Fields (Eds.), *English language learners at school: A guide for administrators* (2nd ed., pp. 207–208). Philadelphia, PA: Caslon Publishing.

Massey, D. S. (2015). Who will the Common Core State Standards serve? How do they reflect 21st century demographic realities? In G. Valdés, K. Menken, & M. Castro (Eds.), *Common core bilingual and English language learners* (pp. 9–10). Philadelphia, PA: Caslon Publishing.

McGee, A., Haworth, P., & Macintyre, L. (2015). Leadership practices to support teaching and learning for English language learners. *TESOL Quarterly, 49*(1), 92–114.

McInnes, J. (Ed.). (1962). The man who kept house. In *Magic and make believe*. Toronto, Canada: Thomas Nelson and Sons.

McNair, J. C. (2010). Classic African American children's literature. *The Reading Teacher, 64*(2), 96–105.

Meek, M. M. (1988). *How texts teach what readers learn*. Stroud, Glos: Thimble Press.

Menosky, D. (1971). *A psycholinguistic description of oral reading miscues generated during the reading of varying portions of text by selected readers from grades two, four, six, and eight*. (Doctoral dissertation). Available from ProQuest Dissertations and Theses database. (UMI No. 7214260).

Mercuri, S., & Ramos, L. (2015). Technology-based biliteracy centers for the 21st century learner. *GIST Education and Learning Research Journal, 9*, 196–216.

Mohan, B. (1990). *LEP students and the integration of language and content: Knowledge structures and tasks*. Washington, D.C.: Proceedings of the First Research Symposium on Limited English Proficient Student Issues.

Moll, L. (1992). Bilingual classroom studies and community analysis. *Educational Researcher, 21*(2), 20–24.

Moll, L. C., & González, N. (1994). Critical issues: Lessons from research with language-minorities children. *Journal of Literacy Research, 26*(4), 429–456.

Moll, L. C., Sáez, R., & Dworin, J. (2001). Exploring biliteracy: Two student case examples of writing as a social practice. *The Elementary School Journal, 101*(4), 435–449.

Morales, A., & Hanson, W. E. (2005). Language brokering: An integrative review of the literature. *Hispanic Journal of Behavioral Sciences, 27*(4), 471–503.

New London Group (1996). A pedagogy of multiliteracies: Designing social futures. *Harvard Educational Review, 66*(1), 60–92.

Nieto, D. (2015). How are students designated as English language learners represented in the Common Core State Standards? In G. Valdés, K. Menken, & M. Castro (Eds.), *Common core bilingual and English language learners* (pp. 13–14). Philadelphia, PA: Caslon Publishing.

Noddings, N. (1984). *Caring: A feminine approach to ethics and moral education*. Berkeley, CA: University of California Press.

Nzai, V. E., Gomez, P., Reyna, C., & Jen, K. (2012). Non-native English speaking elementary ELL teachers' culturally responsive leadership profile in an ESL context. *Colombian Applied Linguistics, 14*(1), 88–108.

O'Dea, C. (2002). Personal communication through shared Teaching Notes.

Office of English Language Acquisition (OELA). (2015). Profiles of English learners (ELs). (Fast Facts). Washington D.C.: U.S. Department of Education. Retrieved from http://www2.ed.gov/about/offices/list/oela/fast-facts/pel.pdf.

Oller, D. K. (2005). ISB4: Proceedings of the 4th International Symposium on Bilingualism, ed. James Cohen, Kara T. McAlister, Kellie Rolstad, and Jeff MacSwan, 1744–1749. Somerville, MA: Cascadilla.

Oller, D. K., Pearson, B. C., & Cobo-Lewis, A. B. (2007). Profile effects in early bilingual language and literacy. *Applied Psycholinguist, 28*(2), 191–230. doi: 10.1017/S0142716407070117.

Olsen, B., & and Kirtman, L. (2002). Teacher as mediator of school reform: An examination of teacher practice in 36 California restructuring schools. *Teachers College Record, 104*(2), 301–324.

Orellana, M., & García, O. (2014). Language brokering and translanguaging in school. *Language Arts, 91*(5), 386–392.

Orellana, M. F., Martínez, D. C., Lee, C. H., & Montaño, E. (2013). "Language as a tool in diverse forms of learning": Corrigendum. *Linguistics and Education, 24*, 272. doi:10.1016/j.linged.2013.01.002.

Ortiz, R. W., & Ordoñez-Jasis, R. (2005). Leyendo juntos (reading together): New directions for Latino parents' early literacy involvement. *The Reading Teacher, 59*, 110–121.

Ovando, C. J. (2003). Bilingual education in the United States: Historical development and current issues. *Bilingual Research Journal, 27*(1), 1–24.

Pacific Policy Research Center. (2010). *Successful bilingual and immersion education models/ programs*. Honolulu: Kamehameha Schools, Research & Evaluation Division.

Palmer, B. C., Chen, C., & Chang, S. (2006). The impact of biculturalism on language and literacy Development: Teaching Chinese English language learners. *Reading Horizons, 46*(4), 239–265.

Paradis, J., Genesee, F., & Crago, M. (2011). *Dual language development and disorders: A handbook on bilingualism and second language learning*. Baltimore, MD: Paul H. Brookes Publishing.

Pearson, B. Z., Fernández, S., & Oller, D. K. (1993). Lexical development in bilingual infants and toddlers: Comparison to monolingual norms. *Language Learning, 43*, 93–120.

Pearson, B. Z., Fernández, S., & Oller, D. K. (1995). Cross language synonyms in the lexicons of bilingual infants: One language or two? *Journal of Child Language, 22*, 345–368.

Pearson, B. Z., & Fernández, S. C. (1994). Patterns of interaction in the lexical development in two languages of bilingual infants. *Language Learning, 44*(4), 617–653.

Pease-Alvarez, L., García, E. E., & Espinosa, P. (1991). Effective instruction for language-minority students: An early childhood case study. *Early Childhood Research Quarterly, 6*, 347–361.

Peters, S. (2010). Literature review: Transition from early childhood education to school. Report for the Ministry of Education. Retrieved from: http://www.educationcounts.govt.nz/publications/ECE/98894/Chapter_4.

Poulin-Dubois, D., Bialystok, E., Blaye, A., Polonia, A., & Yott, J. (2012). Lexical access and vocabulary development in very young bilinguals. *International Journal of Bilingualism*. doi: 1367006911431198.

PowToon (Version 1.1.1) [Online Software]. London, UK: PowToon Limited. *Psycholinguistics, 32*, 333–357. doi: 10.1017/S0142716410000433.

Purdy, J. (2008). Inviting conversation: Meaningful talk about texts for English language learners. *Literacy, 42*(1), 44–51. doi:10.1111/j.1467-9345.2008.00479.x.

Ragan, A., & Lesaux, N. (2006). Federal, state, and district level English language learner program entry and exit requirements: Effects on the education of language minority learners. *Education Policy Analysis Archives, 14*(20). Retrieved from: http://epaa.asu.edu/epaa/v14n20/.

Razfar, A. A. (2012). ¡Vamos a jugar counters! Learning mathematics through funds of knowledge, play, and the third space. *Bilingual Research Journal, 35*(1), 53–75.

Reed, B., & Railsback, J. (2003). Strategies and resources for mainstream teachers of English language learners. *Northwest Regional Educational Laboratory*, 1–43.

Reyes, A., & García, A. (2014). Turnaround policy and practice: A case study of turning around a failing school with English-language-learners. *Urban Revision, 46*, 349–371.

Reyes, M. (2001). Unleashing possibilities: Biliteracy in the primary grades. In M. Reyes & J. Halcón (Eds.), *The best for our children: Critical perspectives on literacy for Latino students*. New York: Teachers College Press.

Reyes, S. A., & Kleyn, T. (2009). *Teaching in two languages: A guide for K–12 bilingual educators*. Thousand Oaks, CA: Corwin Press.

Ricento, T. K., & Hornberger, N. H. (1996). Unpeeling the onion: Language planning and policy and the ELT professional. *TESOL Quarterly, 30*(3), 401–428.

Rinne, L., Gregory, E., Yarmolinskaya, J., & Hardiman, M. (2011). Why arts integration improves long-term retention of content. *Mind, Brain, and Education, 5*(2), 89–96.

Robinson, W. (2009). *Leading people from the middle*. Bloomington, IN: Universe.

Rodríguez, C. C., Filler, J., & Higgins, K. (2012). Using primary language support via computer to improve reading comprehension skills of first-grade English language learners. *Computers in The Schools, 29*(3), 253–267. doi:10.1080/07380569.2012.702718

Rolstad, K., Mahoney, K., & Glass, G. V. (2005). The big picture: A meta analysis of program effectiveness research on English language learners. *Educational Policy, 19*, 572–594.

Rufo, D. (2011). Allowing "artistic agency" in the elementary classroom. *Art Education, 64*(3), 18–23.

Ruiz, R. (March 08, 1984). Orientations in language planning. *Nabe: The Journal for the National Association for Bilingual Education, 8*(2), 15–34.

Sage encyclopedia of human communication sciences and disorders. Thousand Oaks, CA: Sage Publications.

Scanlan, M., & Palmer, D. (2009). Race, power, and (in)equity within two-way immersion settings. *Urban Review, 41*(5), 391–415.

Sebba, M. (2012). Multilingualism in written discourse: An approach to the analysis of multilingual texts. *International Journal of Bilingualism, 17*, 97–118. doi:10.1177/1367006912438301.

Siegel, M., & Panofsky, C. P. (2009). Designs for multi-modality in literacy studies: Explorations in analysis. In K. M. Leander, R. Jimenez, M. Huntley, and V. Risko (Eds.), *58th National Reading Conference Yearbook* (pp. 99–111). Oak Creek, WI: National Reading Conference Inc.

Slavin, R. E., & Cheung, A. (2005). A synthesis of research on language of reading instruction for English language learners. *Review of Educational Research, 75*(2), 247–284.

Snow, C. E., Griffin, P., Burns, M. S., and the NAE Subcommittee on Teaching Reading. (2005). *Knowledge to support the teaching of reading: Preparing teachers for a changing world.* San Francisco, CA: Jossey Bass.

Storybird (Version 1.1.2) [Online software]. Storybird, Inc.

Stritikus, T. (2002). *Immigrant children and the politics of English-only: Views from the classroom.* New York: LFB Scholarly Publishing.

Swinney, R., & Velasco, P. (2011). *Connecting content and academic language for English learners and struggling students, grades 2–6.* Thousand Oaks, CA: Corwin Press.

Talebi, S. H. (2013). Cross-linguistic transfer (from L1 to L2, L2 to L1, and L2 to L3) of reading strategies in a multicompetent mind. *Journal of Language Teaching and Research, 4*(2), 432–436. doi:10.4304/jltr.4.2.432-436.

Thinglink (2015) [Online Software]. Thinglink.

Thomas S., Laccetti J., Mason, B., Mills, S., Perril, S., & Pullinger, K. (2007). Transliteracy: Crossing divides. *First Monday, 12*(2).

Thompson, L. W. (2004). *Literacy development for English language learners: Classroom challenges in the NCLB age.* Monterey, CA: CTB/McGraw Hill.

Tikunoff, W. J., & Vazquez-Faria, J. A. (1982). Successful instruction for bilingual schooling. *Peabody Journal of Education, 59*(4), 234–271.

Torres-Guzmán, M. E., & Goodwin, A. L. (1995). Urban bilingual teachers and mentoring for the future. *Education and Urban Society, 28*, 48–66.

Valdés, G., Menken, K., & Castro, M. (2015). *Common core bilingual and English language learners.* Philadelphia, PA: Caslon Publishing.

Valenzuela, A. (1999). *Subtractive schooling: US-Mexican youth and the politics of caring.* Albany, NY: State University of New York Press.

Velasco, P., & García, O. (2014). Translanguaging and the writing of bilingual learners. *Bilingual Research Journal, 37*(1), 6–23.

VST. (2011). Guidelines for image selection for beginning viewers. Retrieved from www.vtshome.org.

Vygotsky, P. (2002). *Pedagogy of the oppressed.* 30th Anniversary Ed. New York: Continuum.

Watson, D. (2011). Where do we go from here?: From miscues to strategies. In R. Meyer & K. Whitmore (Eds.), *Reclaiming reading: Teachers, students, and researchers regaining spaces for thinking and action* (pp. 67–77). New York: Taylor & Francis/Routledge.

Whitmore, K. F., Martens, P., Goodman, Y. M., & Owocki, G. (December 1, 2004). Critical lessons from the transactional perspective on early literacy research. *Journal of Early Childhood Literacy, 4*(3), 291–325.

WIDA Consortium. (2013). *RtI squared: Developing a culturally and linguistically responsive approach to response to instruction & intervention for English learners.* Madison, WI: Board of Regents of the University of Wisconsin System.

Wiese, A., & García, E. E. (1998). The Bilingual Education Act: Language minority students and equal educational opportunity. *Bilingual Research Journal, 22*(1), 1–18.

Wiley, T. G. (2015). In what ways are the Common Core State Standards de facto language education policy? In G. Valdés, K. Menken, & M. Castro (Eds.), *Common core bilingual and English language learners* (pp. 10–11). Philadelphia, PA: Caslon Publishing.

Wiley, T.G., & Rolstad, K. (2014). The Common Core State Standards and the great divide. *International Multilingual Research Journal, 8,* 1–18.

Wong Fillmore, L., & Martinez, R. B. (2015). Content are language demands. In G. Valdés, K. Menken, & M. Castro (Eds.), *Common core bilingual and English language learners* (pp. 155–161). Philadelphia, PA: Caslon Publishing.

Yenawine, P. (1999). Theory into practice: The visual thinking strategies. Paper presented at the Aesthetic and Art Education: A Transdisciplinary Approach Conference, Calouste Gulbenkian Foundation. Lisbon, Portugal.

Yenawine, P. (2003). *Visual thinking strategies: Using art to deepen learning across school disciplines.* Cambridge, MA: Harvard Education Press.

Yenawine, P. (2005). Thoughts on visual literacy. In J. Flood, S. B. Hecht, & D. Lapp (Eds.), *Handbook of research on teaching literacy through the communicative arts* (pp. 485–486). Mahwah, NJ: Lawrence Erlbaum.

Yoon, B., Simpson, A., & Haag, C. (2010). Assimilation ideology: Critically examining underlying messages in multicultural literature. *Journal of Adolescent & Adult Literacy, 54*(2), 109–118.

Zwiers, J. (2007). *Building academic language: Essential practices for content classrooms.* San Francisco: Jossey-Bass.

About the Editor

Dr. Mayra C. Daniel, a professor in the Department of Curriculum and Instruction at Northern Illinois University, is the coordinator for the Bilingual / English as a Second Language Program for NIU's College of Education. She recently finished serving as an elected member of the TESOL Organization's Nominating Committee. She has been chair of several committees of the International Literacy Association, such as the Literacy, Diversity, and Multiculturalism Committee.

Daniel's research and teaching center on preparing and empowering educators who work with plurilingual and pluricultural learners in the United States, Guatemala, and Ecuador. She is committed to helping teachers plan culturally responsive instruction and become advocates for English learners and their communities. In her work, she has focused on formative assessment, bilingual education, technology in literacy, and instructional methodologies for classrooms with English learners.

She has presented her research at numerous national and international conferences. Three of her more recent publications are book chapters that address the topics of social justice, cultural capital in English-language teaching, and preparing novice teachers to work with English learners: Critical Pedagogy's Power in English Language Teaching and Exploring Perceptions of Gender Roles in English Language Teaching (In L. R. Jacobs and C. Hastings, *The Importance of Social Justice in English Language Teaching*, 2016), and Planning Instruction for English Language Learners: Strategies Teachers Need to Know (In D. Schwarzer and J. Grinberg, *Successful Teaching: What Every Novice Teacher Needs to Know*, 2016, Rowman & Littlefield). In 2015, she coedited *Research-Based Instruction That Makes a Difference in English Learners' Success* (Rowman & Littlefield).

Contributors

Kelly Allen, University of Arizona
Ester de Jong, University of Florida
Yetta Goodman, University of Arizona
Barbara E. Marler, Skokie School District #68
Aida A. Nevárez-La Torre, Fordham University
Carol Owles, Illinois State University
Tuba Yilmaz, University of Florida

www.ingramcontent.com/pod-product-compliance
Lightning Source LLC
Chambersburg PA
CBHW021850300426
44115CB00005B/104